For Better

by

Eric Coble

D1522838

NEW YORK HOLLYWOOD LONDON TORONTO

SAMUELFRENCH.COM

ISBN 978-0-573-66398-7   Printed in U.S.A.   #8227

IMPORTANT BILLING AND CREDIT REQUIREMENTS
All producers of *FOR BETTER must* give credit to the Author of the Play in all programs distributed in connection with performances of the Play, and in all instances in which the title of the Play appears for the purposes of advertising, publicizing or otherwise exploiting the Play and/or a production. The name of the Author *must* appear on a separate line on which no other name appears, immediately following the title and *must* appear in size of type not less than fifty percent of the size of the title type.

For Better was originally commissioned by Curious Theatre Company, Chip Walton, Producing Artistic Director. This Commission was funded in part by a grant from the National New Play Network

The world premiere of **FOR BETTER** was produced by Curious Theatre Company in Denver, CO on November 3, 2007. It was directed by Chip Walton with the following cast and crew:

MICHAEL	John Arp
LIZZIE	Rhonda Brown
STUART	Ed Cord
FRANCINE	Dee Covington
KAREN	Lisa Rosenhagen
WALLY	Jim Zeiger

Set by Michael Durna, Lights by Richard Devin, Costumes by Brynn Coplan, Sound design by Brian Freeland, Properties by Jennifer Orell, Assistant Directed by Pesha Rudnick, Stage Managed by Lisa Boehm and Assistant Stage Managed by Paul Turley.

FOR BETTER opened November 8, 2007 at New Theatre, Coral Gables, FL; Ricky Martinez, Artistic Director; Eileen Suarez, Managing Director. It was directed by Ricky Martinez. The cast was as follows:

WALLY	Kevin Reilley
KAREN	Kay Ostrenko
FRANCINE	Kim Ostrenko
MICHAEL	Christopher Vicchiollo
STUART	John Manzelli
LIZZIE	Evelyn Perez

Set by Jesse Dreikosen, Costumes by K. Blair Brown, Lights by Patrick Tennent, Sound by Clint Hooper.

FOR BETTER opened April 2, 2008 at Southern Rep, New Orleans, LA; Ryan Rylette, Producing Artistic Director; Aimee Hayes, Artistic Director. It was directed by Gary Rucker. The cast was as follows:

WALLY	George Sanchez
KAREN	Ashley Ricord
FRANCINE	Aimee Hayes
MICHAEL	Leon Contavesprie
STUART	Sean Patterson
LIZZIE	Veronica Russell

Set by David Raphel, Lights by Marty Sachs, Costumes by Elizabeth Parent, Sound by Michael Singleton.

CHARACTERS

WALLY BAEDEKER. A Man Who's Been Married; Karen's Father, 60's.
KAREN BAEDEKER. A Woman Who Wants to Be, 30's.
FRANCINE DEXTER. A Woman Who Is Married; Karen's Sister, 40's.
MICHAEL DEXTER. The Man Francine Married, 40's.
STUART TRAMONTANE. A Man Who is Buffeted, 30's.
LIZZIE MONOHAN. A Woman Who Floats, 30's.

PLACE

Various locales across the globe.

TIME

Now.

PRODUCTION NOTES

FOR BETTER is meant to be performed by SIX actors of any ethnic group. The scenes should be staged in as many different areas and levels of the theatre as possible – including in the audience – with Wally's couch and living room the only stable focal point.

For lighting
- Floor lamp near French doors
- Floor lamps stage rt. near living room
- lamp near bathroom (stage lft)
- lights over Island
- light for main living room

- get rid of palms p23
p21

To remember:
- Never look at anyone
  when on phones.
✗ wherever there is a conversation there is light
- Turn your light on when you
  enter + turn it off when you
  leave
- Handle pictures and other
  functions as you normally
  would on your phone. (swipes)

(**SETTING:** *A mostly bare stage representing various locations around the world.*)

(**AT RISE:** *A woman in a business suit,* **KAREN BAEDE-KER,** *stands beside her father,* **WALLY,** *in a bathrobe and slippers next to a well-worn couch and end table with an old phone sitting on it.*)

(*This is* **WALLY***'s living room.*)

WALLY. Does it have to be here and now?

KAREN. My plane leaves in two hours, Dad, I want to talk face to face –

WALLY. – cause you know I'd do anything for you.

KAREN. I know.

WALLY. – but my programs are coming on.

KAREN. I know.

WALLY. It's "Kojak" and "Rockford Files," sweetheart. Back to back. It's the centerpiece of my day.

KAREN. That's what the TiVo is for, Dad, so we can have talks like this *and* you can get your shows.

WALLY. That's a good point. That's true. Except the TiVo thing is still kind of in the box.

KAREN. Why didn't you hook it up?

WALLY. Oh, you know, those damn instructions –

KAREN. I would've hooked it up, you could've called me to set it up –

WALLY. My Karie's got nothing better to do than hook up her old man's gizmos –

KAREN. Where is it? Where's the box?

WALLY. Over by the door where the UPS guy left it.

KAREN. Dad!

WALLY. I'm uncomfortable with it, Karie. You want me to say it, there I said it. TiVo scares me.

7

KAREN. Oh, Dad –

WALLY. The VCR was bad enough, honey, it'd come clicking on recording at all hours of the night on the wrong days – it's like I got ghosts in my house, whatdoyoucallem, poltergeists, Karie. I already got enough spirits following me without some damn machine whirring away –

KAREN. TiVo's silent. You'll never know it's here –

WALLY. It stays in the box, I'll never know it's here either.

KAREN. Okay. This is a different conversation, we can have this conversation when I get back – right now I need to tell you something.

WALLY. What if you tell me and I have the T.V. on at the same time?

KAREN. Dad, please.

WALLY. I'll mute it. Just the picture.

KAREN. Dad!

(WALLY *pauses. Looks at the remote in his hand. At his daughter. Smiles and puts the remote down as he sits.*)

WALLY. I saw these shows when they came on the first time, you'd think I didn't need to see 'em again.

KAREN. *(sitting beside him)* But they were good shows.

WALLY. They *were* good shows. Those were shows you could *watch*. Your mother and I, we *watched* those shows. She loved James Garner. Loved him.

KAREN. *(wiping her eyes)* I know.

WALLY. What. What's wrong? I'm sorry. Sweetheart, I'm sorry, we'll do the TiVo. You come back and show me how –

KAREN. No. No! It's just… I wish Mom was here.

(*Beat.* WALLY *sits again.*)

WALLY. Yeah. Me too.

(KAREN *looks at her watch, pulls out her cell phone and sets it on the couch between them. They wait.* WALLY *looks at the phone…*)

WALLY. *(continued)* You're... you're not expecting Mom to call us are you?

KAREN. No! But I am expecting a call.

WALLY. I thought we were going to have a talk.

KAREN. We are. Right after the call. The call is for you.

WALLY. Oh, Jesus, Dr. Lehman got the results back, didn't he? It's not just hemorrhoids, is it? Oh god, oh Jesus –

KAREN. No, Dad!

WALLY. He said more fiber – you all said more fiber, but did I listen?

KAREN. It's not Dr. Lehman! Dr. Lehman wouldn't be calling me, he'd call you and he said he's 99% sure it was nothing, right?

WALLY. 99% – he did say 99% –

KAREN. Dad, this isn't medical. This call is good news. 100% good news.

WALLY. Holy Pete. My whole life was flashing before my eyes.

KAREN. I'm sorry.

WALLY. You ever have that happen? Whoosh, flash –

KAREN. No, no, I haven't.

WALLY. Well, yours would be shorter. You know.

KAREN. I know.

(KAREN *looks at her watch. Checks her phone.*)

WALLY. They late?

KAREN. A little late. Probably caught in a meeting. But he knows I have to get to the airport...

WALLY. Why is someone calling me on your phone?

KAREN. You'll see.

(*They wait. Looking at the phone...*KAREN *looks at her watch.*)

He's usually really punctual.

WALLY. He who.

KAREN. Max. Max Aphelion.

WALLY. Ah. *(beat)* And Max Aphelion is not a doctor.

KAREN. Not at all.*(beat)* I think he's my fiancé.

   (**WALLY** *stares at her*).

   I'm getting married, Dad.

   (**WALLY** *stares at her.*)

   Is that okay?

   (He stands, sits, stands.)

WALLY. Oh!...Karen. Oh. Karen. Karen! Oh! This is –

KAREN. Are you okay with it?

WALLY. Oh, sweetheart – this is worth missing "Kojak" for!

   (He hugs her, she's laughing.)

   Sweetheart!

KAREN. Is it great?

WALLY. Oh god! Sweetheart!

KAREN. It's great, isn't it?

WALLY. I didn't know you were seeing anyone!

KAREN. I wasn't! We just met – not *just* met, we met at the International Retail Foods Conference in Tampa last year and we've only seen each other twice since then, but we talk everyday – multiple times everyday – I haven't actually seen him in two months but he asked me to marry him! He proposed! Which is so like him once you get to know him – he just does it, he thinks, he does it – everyone else in food management is so "stay with the itinerary," "stick to the Power Point," but he's all instinct, and his instinct was to fall in love and mine was too and his instinct was to propose and mine was to accept, I think, I mean, I think it's okay, right, and he's calling you to ask for my hand in marriage, your permission –

WALLY. Wow.

KAREN. He's very old-fashioned. Impulsive and old-fash-ioned. Be nice to him, please be nice to him!

WALLY. Of course I'm gonna be nice, but why doesn't he, he could drop by. I could make some Stouffer's Macaroni –

KAREN. He's in Montreal until Tuesday. But he was going to call at 1:15. I don't know why he hasn't called...

WALLY. You only met him twice?

KAREN. But we talk every day, and send pictures, text messages – I see him and hear him more than I see anyone else I know – here –

(showing her cell phone screen)

Here's what he looks like. This was in the Tampa Airport right before I flew to Detroit and he went to Istanbul.

WALLY. His head's a little big.

KAREN. That's the angle of the phone camera. Here's him in Turkey. He e-mailed me these photos –

(pushing buttons)

In Seattle. Sao Paolo. Houston.

WALLY. You sure he's not a drug runner?

KAREN. I don't think so. No! Why? Do you think he is?

WALLY. A mule or whatever they call'em?

KAREN. He works for Starbucks.

WALLY. He can't hold down a job at the one on the corner?

KAREN. He's in management. He's a scout. A location scout for new Starbucks all over the world.

WALLY. Oh well, that's probably a real interesting job.

KAREN. You should read his letters.

WALLY. And he's a looker.

KAREN. You think so? I think so.

WALLY. No, his head's not that big or nothing. He's a good lookin' man.

KAREN. I don't know why he hasn't called –

(dialing)

I'll call him –

WALLY. It's kind of neat, you're both in food service. Sort of. Gives you something to talk about. Your mother and I, we'd talk about my construction jobs, you know, but after a few years pouring concrete in one high-rise is pouring concrete in any high-rise, you know? But she'd listen, you know –

KAREN. *(into phone)* Hey, Max, it's Karen. I'm at my dad's but I'm heading to the airport in a minute so....I was just wondering if you'd be calling. Hope everything's okay. I love you. Bye.

(She hangs up. Looks at **WALLY**. *Pause.)*

WALLY. You love him?

KAREN. He, um, I was eating breakfast at the hotel and he just walked up and sat down beside me. There were no other tables available, it was the Sheraton Buffet Breakfast, which is always crowded, and we started talking about coffee and branding and seating capacity and we were both laughing, and he has these great eyes and this laugh, it's like a snort, but cute – and I just had the urge to touch him. To hold his hand or something, I wanted to feel him...and I'm thinking how wildly inappropriate, as usual, I am – and I focus on my orange juice and he reaches over...and takes my hand. Just for a minute. Less than a minute. Without saying anything. He just wanted to touch me. And then he gets up to get me more hash browns and we spent the whole rest of the day talking and walking... And we've been kind of doing that ever since. *(beat)*

WALLY. Then you better get to the airport. Give him my number. Have him call me. I want to welcome him to the family.

(She hugs him, practically bouncing.)

KAREN. Oh, thank you thank you thank you, you think it's okay?

WALLY. Will you stop asking that? Do *you* think it's okay?

KAREN. Of course! I think. Maybe he can e-mail you his proposal–

WALLY. No e-mails. I do not do e-mails.

KAREN. Right. Sorry. I forgot.

WALLY. With the little smiley faces, winking, frowning, it's like trying to read a goddam cartoon telegram.

KAREN. He'll call you –

WALLY. Have you told your sister?

KAREN. *(takes his hand)* I wanted to do it with you.

(**WALLY** *stands beside* **KAREN** *while she dials, barely keeping it together – wriggling in place…*)

(Then another woman in business clothes, **FRANCINE**, *wheels into a different area in an office chair with her laptop, answering her cell phone.)*

FRANCINE. *(into phone)* Hello?

KAREN. Francine – Oh, Francie, Francie, Francie, Francie –

FRANCINE. Karen? Is that you? Are you okay?

KAREN. Ohmygod, ohmygod, ohmygod, ohmygod –

WALLY. You're gonna hyperventilate, you better sit down –

FRANCINE. You need to hang up and call 911, or I'll call it for you, where are you?

KAREN. It's gonna happen, Daddy said it's really gonna happen so it's gonna happen –

FRANCINE. Did Dr. Lehman call? What's going on?

KAREN. He proposed! I mean he hasn't called back yet but he proposed!

FRANCINE. Dad proposed? To who?

KAREN. Max! Max asked me to marry him! Max and me, me and Max –

FRANCINE. Do we know a Max?

KAREN. Max from Starbucks!

FRANCINE. You're marrying a guy you just met at Starbucks?

KAREN. He works for Starbucks! Isn't it great? Oh my god, I think I'm getting married, Francine, I'm getting married, I'm getting married –

FRANCINE. Hang on, wait, I've got another call –

(A man in a suit, tie and easy smile, wheels into a different area in a rolling chair, holding a steering wheel and talking into his cell phone. This is **MICHAEL**.)

MICHAEL. *(into phone, to* **FRANCINE***)* Hey, Sweets, where are you?

FRANCINE. Oh my god, Michael honey, Karen's getting married.

KAREN. *(to herself as* **WALLY** *tries to seat her)* I'm getting married I'm getting married I'm getting married –

MICHAEL. Karen?

FRANCINE. Getting married.

MICHAEL. She met somebody on the road?

FRANCINE. At a Starbucks.

WALLY. It's gonna be fine, it's gonna be fine, it's gonna be fine –

MICHAEL. I think I missed that, I thought you said Starbucks –

FRANCINE. Where are you – can I call you back?

MICHAEL. I didn't think your sister even went to Starbucks –

FRANCINE. *(punching a button on her phone, To* **KAREN***)* What Starbucks was this?

KAREN. I didn't meet him in Starbucks – he works for Starbucks.

FRANCINE. What?

*(***STUART***, a man in a windbreaker and jeans jogs into a different area with a map and cell phone.)*

MICHAEL. *(into phone)* What.

STUART. Hello, Michael, it's Stuart, can you hear me?

MICHAEL. Long time no contact, dude. Where are you?

STUART. In the field, wanted to see if my phone could reach you from here. I'm in a ravine –

KAREN. He's based in the Midwest Headquarters in St. Louis.

STUART. I'm in Kyrgyzstan. Somewhere.

FRANCINE. *(to* **KAREN***)* Are you in St. Louis?

KAREN. I'm at Dad's. Max called me and I came to see Dad –

FRANCINE. He proposed over the phone?

MICHAEL. Guess who just got proposed to?

STUART. Did you say proposed?

MICHAEL & FRANCINE. Karen!

KAREN & STUART. What?

FRANCINE. What do you know about this guy?

STUART. Karen Baedeker?

KAREN. Max Aphelion. Isn't that a great name? He's great, Francine, I think you'll love him, I hope you'll love him, he's funny and sweet and smart –

FRANCINE & STUART. You're kidding me.

KAREN & MICHAEL. I think it's kind of great.

KAREN. I've been alone for so long.

MICHAEL. She's been alone for so long.

FRANCINE. Wait, I've got another call. Hang on –

(A woman in comfy clothes walks into a different area with her cell phone. This is LIZZIE.)

LIZZIE. *(to FRANCINE)* Hello, Francie-Pants, where are you?

FRANCINE. Hi, Lizzie –

STUART. Are you driving? 'Cause you're fading in and out –

MICHAEL. I'm driving.

FRANCINE. I'm in San Diego, Karen's on the other line, I think you need to talk to her –

LIZZIE. I'm trying on new contacts, I was wondering what color eyes I should have today –

MICHAEL. Can you hear me now? I'm out from under the overpass –

STUART. I just sort of can't believe she's getting married.

FRANCINE. *(to LIZZIE)* I'm hooking up a conference call –

LIZZIE. Francine –

KAREN. Lizzie?

MICHAEL. Can you hear me now?

STUART. I can hear you now.

FRANCINE. Can the three of us hear each other?

LIZZIE. Karen, I'm trying on contacts, what color eyes do you think I should have today?

KAREN. Lizzie, I'm getting married!

LIZZIE. What?

STUART. She wasn't even seeing anyone last time we talked –

MICHAEL. Yeah, but when was that?

LIZZIE. When did this happen?

KAREN. Just now.

STUART. Two months ago.

KAREN. His name is Max Aphelion – he just proposed.

LIZZIE. *(squeals and claps)* OH Karen Karen Karen Karen Karen –

FRANCINE. Oh god.

MICHAEL. *(overlapping)* A lot can happen in two months, buddy. Anyway, what do you care?

MICHAEL & KAREN. Isn't it great?

LIZZIE. Yes, it's great!!   **STUART.** Yeah, it's great.
It's…wow!!   It's wow.

LIZZIE. "Max Aphelion," what a great name –

FRANCINE. I want to know more about this guy.

MICHAEL. I'm losing you.

KAREN. Francine, will you help me pick out a wedding dress?

LIZZIE. I'll help you get a dress!

KAREN. Francine, will you help me pick a dress?

LIZZIE. I would so love to pick out a dress!

MICHAEL. I'm between some buildings –

LIZZIE. I'm between phones, guys, my battery's going – I have to hang up –

KAREN. What? I couldn't hear you.

STUART. Can you hear me now?

FRANCINE. Karen, I have to run. I'll call you tonight –

LIZZIE & MICHAEL. Can you hear me?

KAREN. Just say "congratulations," Francie, please, just say "congratulations" –

STUART. I'm losing you –

LIZZIE. Congratulations, Karen!

FRANCINE. I'm losing you, Lizzie.

MICHAEL. I'm losing you, Stuart.

KAREN. Did you hear me, Francie?

LIZZIE & STUART. Can you hear me now?

KAREN. Please just say "congratulations"?

LIZZIE & STUART & MICHAEL. Can you hear me?

KAREN. Please?

LIZZIE, KAREN, STUART, MICHAEL & FRANCINE. Can you hear me?

ALL. I'm hanging up.

(They do. Beat. KAREN *turns to face her father.)*

WALLY. Did she say congratulations?

KAREN. I, um, I have to get to the airport. I'll call you.

(A quick hug and she darts out. WALLY *follows her.* LIZZIE *and* STUART *exit as* FRANCINE *redials* MICHAEL.)*

FRANCINE. Michael, honey.

MICHAEL. Hey, babe. That's awesome about Karen – I'll give her a jingle –

FRANCINE. Awesome? She has one good Frappuccino Grande and she starts hearing wedding bells –

MICHAEL. Honey, if she says she's in love –

FRANCINE. It's a fine line between love and desperation.

MICHAEL. Well, sure.

FRANCINE. Karen's not even looking down to see where that line is – somebody's gotta look down, Michael.

MICHAEL. Absolutely.

FRANCINE. Will you Google Max Aphelion and Starbucks and see what you find?

MICHAEL. I'm on my way to a client.

FRANCINE. So am I! I'm going into a group in two minutes –

MICHAEL. What's the focus?

FRANCINE. It's for Charles Schwab. They want to see if people want to invest more when they see a picture of a mountain, the ocean, or a wheat field.

MICHAEL. Mountain. Totally.

FRANCINE. Why.

MICHAEL. Steady. Solid. Forever.

FRANCINE. Does it matter if it's a blue sky or overcast behind the mountain?

MICHAEL. Overcast means storm, means we'll stand through wind and rain.

FRANCINE. Birds in the sky flying toward the mountain.

MICHAEL. Distracting. I'm not putting my IRA in birds.

FRANCINE. But people looking at the ocean photo feel sexier and more daring, more willing to take risks.

MICHAEL. I can see that.

FRANCINE. So we're testing responses to a big phallic island in the ocean. Best of both worlds – maybe a couple of subliminal dolphins mating in the waves.

MICHAEL. Then they should have prairie dogs humping in the wheat field.

FRANCINE. And that's why I don't invite you to my focus groups. And this has nothing to do with the crisis at hand, Michael. I need the 411 on Max Aphelion. I think she said something about St. Louis –

MICHAEL. I can do some fishing this afternoon –

FRANCINE. Or get Lizzie. She's better on the web than all of us combined.

MICHAEL. Lizzie Monohan?

FRANCINE. You know another Lizzie?

MICHAEL. She's your friend, talking to her is your job, not mine.

FRANCINE. I was just on the line with her when her cell went out – you'll have to use her landline – do you have her landline?

MICHAEL. Not if she's moved since our wedding...

FRANCINE. She's moved six times since then. I'll text it to you if you don't. Get her sniffing around, sil vous plait. I'll call you after my group, love you, bye!

(And she leaves. MICHAEL hangs up, steers, looks at his phone and redials. LIZZIE re-enters carrying a laptop and checking out contact lenses, with her phone cord stretching offstage.) use land line phone

LIZZIE. Hello?

MICHAEL. Lizzie! It's Michael! How you doin'?

LIZZIE. Michael! Oh my god! How are you? Which Michael is this? James spot otega nt

MICHAEL. Michael Dexter.

LIZZIE. Michael! Oh my god! How are you? It's been for-ever! How'd you get my landline?

MICHAEL. Francine had it.

LIZZIE. Oh that is so cool that you guys still talk. I know so many people – married people – who just don't talk anymore, you know?

MICHAEL. I know –

LIZZIE. Or wives who don't let their husbands talk to other women, or you know, former lovers or whatever, jeal-ously is such a hideous monster, don't you think?

MICHAEL. Absolutely.

LIZZIE. Are you driving? It sounds like you're driving?

MICHAEL. I am driving –

LIZZIE. Where are you? Oh my god, are you in town? You're not driving to my house, are you? Tell me you're not driving to my house, it is such a sty –

MICHAEL. I'm not driving to your house. Not unless you moved to the Gentle Hearth Retirement Community in Tulsa.

LIZZIE. No, I've never been to Tulsa. Is it beautiful? Is it flat? Does it smell?

MICHAEL. Why would it smell?

LIZZIE. Are you looking at retiring there? I thought you were from Denver? Won't you go back to Denver to die, like salmon swimming back upstream?

MICHAEL. I'm with Advantage Plus –

LIZZIE. That's right! Francie told me – you're in insurance!

MICHAEL. Just for satellite dishes. We only offer policies on dishes and cable lines.

LIZZIE. And the old people want their satellite dishes insured?

MICHAEL. I sure as hell hope so.

LIZZIE. That is so cool that you take care of the entertain-ment needs of our elders. I love that.

MICHAEL. You still with Amazon?

LIZZIE. God no, I'm strictly E-Bay now.

MICHAEL. Ah.

LIZZIE. I make sure the seller ratings are up-to-date and accurate.

MICHAEL. Wow.

LIZZIE. It's huge. It's like being an air traffic controller, except here people's lives are at stake, you know?

MICHAEL. Are you on the job now?

LIZZIE. I don't have to check every second, Michael. It's like being a dominatrix. You just kind of hover, watching intently, listening for clues, ready to swing your metal-studded paddle at just the right moment. You know?

(Beat. MICHAEL *drives.* LIZZIE *sits.)*

MICHAEL. Um. So you, ah, your house is still a sty, huh?

LIZZIE. Please. If I wouldn't clean it up when you were around, you think I'll dust when I'm on my own?

MICHAEL. Right.

(Pause. He drives. She bites her lip and types.)

LIZZIE. So you like it? Advantage Plus?

MICHAEL. It's got solid bennies. Nobody watching my every move, you know.

LIZZIE. Yeah, you always had that sneaky element –

MICHAEL. I'm not sneaky –

LIZZIE. Stealthy spy-boy thing. Back when we were together – before you even met Francine, you were still always like, "I wonder if I can get away with this?"

MICHAEL. Look who's talking!

LIZZIE. Well, but see, it never occurred to me that anything I did was wrong, so I never snuck. Are you sneaking now?

MICHAEL. No! Francine asked me to call! She wants you to check on –

LIZZIE. Karen! Oh my god, that's right, of course she would, isn't that wonderful? I mean not the suspicious, doubting Thomas pessimist thing, but the true love thing, the Karen getting married thing!

MICHAEL. It's a fine line between love and desperation, Lizzie, and I'm not sure Karen's looking down right now.

LIZZIE. What?

MICHAEL. Francine's just – we're both just worried she doesn't know what she's getting into.

LIZZIE. It's just marriage. It's not like buying a car.

MICHAEL. Exactly. Just picture every time Karen's ever bought a car, except there's no lemon laws to bail her out this time.

LIZZIE. She sounded so happy in the eight seconds we were on the phone together –

MICHAEL. And we want her to stay happy. Can you just snoop around a little – see who Max Aphelion out of St. Louis Starbucks HQ is.

LIZZIE. Like criminal records?

MICHAEL. Sexual harassments, embezzlement, xeroxing his private parts –

LIZZIE. What's wrong with xeroxing your private parts?

MICHAEL. You can't just go throwing love to just anybody – if Karen won't protect her heart, it's up to us.

LIZZIE. It sounds like her heart's already gone. All we can do now is try to shove the oozing thing back into her empty chest cavity.

MICHAEL. I think we're all praying that won't be necessary.

(parks his car)

I'm at my meeting. Will you check? Please?

LIZZIE. …I'll report back to Francine.

MICHAEL. Or I'll call you. Or you call me. You know.

LIZZIE. Just like old times. Say hello to the old people.

(She hangs up…pauses…and walks out. **MICHAEL** *hangs up and walks off as* **STUART** *trots into a different area with a map and dialling his cell phone.* **KAREN** *enters in still another area with a rolling suitcase, answering her cell.)*

KAREN. Hello, this is Karen.

STUART. Karen! Hey, it's Stuart. Can you hear me?

KAREN. Stuart! How are you? Where are you?

STUART. I'm sort of in Kyrgyzstan.

KAREN. Wow. The reception sounds pretty good there.

STUART. I drove back into Bishkek to call you. I'm supposed to be in the countryside to test our range there today and tomorrow.

KAREN. That's so cool.

STUART. Yeah. Yeah, it is. I just wish I liked goat wool better. Where are you?

KAREN. Airport to Santa Fe. There's a Hometown Buffet there that's getting a four on its customer evaluations – I'm going in to monitor for three days.

STUART. Well, ah, a little goat tells me you've got some other news!

KAREN. Oh my god, who told you? I just told my dad and you're hearing it in Kazakhstan?

STUART. Kyrgyzstan. It's a bit closer. You know. Michael Dexter told me. He's pretty much my best phone-buddy now – we test reception, shoot the breeze, he tells me when one of my best friends suddenly gets engaged. You know. So congratulations.

KAREN. Thank you, Stuart. Thank you so much.

STUART. So is this someone in the Hometown Buffet family? A nice president in charge of pork loins or something?

KAREN. Starbucks. He's a Starbucks scout.

STUART. Oh good lord.

KAREN. Is that bad?

STUART. No! I mean it could be worse. He could work for the death squads in Sudan.

KAREN. Well, you're not working for a mom-and-pop yourself, Mr. Verizon.

STUART. That's true. I just have this nagging fear everytime I leave my apartment that when I get back there'll be a new Starbucks in my kitchen.

KAREN. I'm glad you called.

STUART. Well, I had to find out if I'd heard right or if it was a static burst that sounded like "wedding." But you're getting married! Karen Baedeker is getting married!

KAREN. I think it's really happening. I just spoke to Max – he's calling my father now – he got tied up in a conference call earlier – he's really old-fashioned –

STUART. That's great. Sort of like me.

KAREN. Exactly. He's funny, self-deprecating –

STUART. Sounds like someone we know!

KAREN. He goes all over the world, he's just fascinated with local customs and people –

STUART. Bing Bing! Three for three!

KAREN. We're just such a great great fit.

STUART. And he had the nerve to pop the question! Three cheers for him! Hip Hip –

KAREN & STUART. – Hooray!

KAREN. We're e-mailing invitations ASAP. Not that many, we both want a small wedding, but you'll be first on the list –

STUART. Maybe I could be the Maid of Honor or something.

KAREN. You should go ahead and get the date in your ~~Palm~~ – *calendar* ~~numbers cell~~

STUART. (~~gets out his PDA~~) I can do up to 200 years in advance – when are you thinking?

KAREN. Fifteen days from today.

STUART. Oh dear god.

KAREN. We wanted to give everyone two weeks to get the best ticket prices – can you make it – I know it's short notice –

STUART. That's certainly one phrase that leaps to mind –

KAREN. It's okay, isn't it? I want to get married at home and he's got an appointment only 150 miles away that day – he can drive up –

STUART. Karen, I really think – I mean far be it from me to actually impose an opinion on anyone, but I don't think this is a good idea –

KAREN. What? You're breaking up.

STUART. Stupid Kyrgyzstan!

(moving several steps away)

Can you hear me now?

KAREN. What? Stuart, are you still there?

STUART. *(hopping from spot to spot)* Karen, listen – okay, because, ever since that first day in college, that first Lit class where you spilled coffee on my book –

KAREN. Stuart?

STUART. Can you hear me? Karen, I've never told you this – but –

KAREN. *(yelling into phone)* I'll call you later, Stuart!

*(She hangs up and **STUART** slams shut his own phone.)* or punch phone

STUART. *(yelling to Heaven)* DAMN YOU, KYRGYZSTAN!

*(Lights shift – **STUART** flees as **KAREN** hits a button on her phone and **WALLY** walks on stringing his long phone cord behind him.)*

WALLY. Karen, honey.

KAREN. Hi, Dad.

WALLY. Well, I talked to your beaux, I think he was in Toronto. He asked for your hand.

KAREN. …And?

WALLY. Well, there's a way of talking, you know? The way some people can just put the talking and the spaces between the talking together – especially on a phone – that just make you feel…like they hear you. Like they like hearing you. Your Uncle Hank did that. It's like a good solid handshake and a look in the eye, except through a tiny little wire a hundred miles away, you know.

KAREN. …and?

WALLY. Your Max has a good handshake.

KAREN. Thank you.

*(**KAREN** and **WALLY** exit in opposite directions as **LIZZIE** and **FRANCINE** come on in chairs, holding laptops, talking on their phones.)*

Stage I new island

FRANCINE. Thank you, Lizzie.

LIZZIE. Oh, hey, no prob.

FRANCINE. I don't think Karen's malicious. I just don't think she thinks! She's such a grasshopper, always leaving it up to us ants to think further ahead than tonight –

LIZZIE. I've always been partial to dung beetles – working and working to take a load of poop and roll it into a tidy ball and roll it home to play with –

FRANCINE. They don't play with the poop, Lizzie. They eat it.

(beat)

LIZZIE. What?

FRANCINE. They digest it over several days. It's not a toy.

LIZZIE. Eww.

FRANCINE. Yeah.

LIZZIE. Then I don't like that bug much at all. I mean I'm sure it's okay for them, but for me, that's just kind of unpleasant –

FRANCINE. But the point is, at least she has you and me to take care of her – and as far as you can tell –

LIZZIE. There are no red flags on her Max Aphelion. Though there's a Max Aphelion on the city council in Wapakaneta who keeps introducing measures to outlaw children on public property. He seems unpopular.

FRANCINE. I may keep digging around.

LIZZIE. It's kind of a race against the clock, isn't it? You only have two weeks to run a security clearance –

FRANCINE. Twelve days.

LIZZIE. What?

FRANCINE. We only have twelve days left until the wedding. Another typical Karen move.

LIZZIE. Well, if I were her I'd want to have the wedding when the groom was in town too.

FRANCINE. And this is the only time in the next year? He can't take vacation days?

LIZZIE. Maybe he hasn't accrued enough.

FRANCINE. Why are you making excuses for this mistake?

LIZZIE. Why are you so hostile to this mistake?

FRANCINE. I'm not hostile! I'm worried! I'm careful! I'm full of care!

LIZZIE. Well, do you want to relay my private eye work to Michael or should I?

FRANCINE. Why?

LIZZIE. He asked me to call him with what I found out.

FRANCINE. No, I'll call him later. When we're back at our hotels.

LIZZIE. Where are you?

FRANCINE. I'm in Sacramento testing groups on different mayoral candidates and slogans.

LIZZIE. Excellent! Anything good?

FRANCINE. We're getting big reactions to "Re-Elect Dan Schultz: Ending Corruption is the Least of His Talents."

LIZZIE. You're amazing!

FRANCINE. If something's worth doing, it's worth doing right, you know?

LIZZIE. You are like, the most diligent person I know.

FRANCINE. Thank you.

(Her phone buzzes.)

Hang on.

(KAREN scoots on in a rolling chair, opening her laptop, talking on her cell.) stage 1st

Karen?

KAREN. Hi, Francine! Sorry I'm late.

FRANCINE. I've got Lizzie on the other line. Hold on.

(pushes a button on her phone)

Can we all hear each other?

LIZZIE. Hi, Karie!

KAREN. Hi, Lizzie, thank you so much – both of you – for doing this. I woke up this morning thinking this is the kind of thing a mother is supposed to do – but you know...I just...I really –

LIZZIE. I consider it a deep honor and privilege to be your mother this afternoon, Karie.

KAREN. Thank you.

(looks at her ~~PDA~~ Calouder or Cell

Oh my gosh. I just got a text from Max!

LIZZIE. What's it say?

KAREN. He's in a warm bath…it's a list of where he wants to kiss me…left shoulder…line of the neck…

LIZZIE. He works his way down?

KAREN. …oh yes.

LIZZIE. I'm getting all wiggly!

KAREN. There is nothing hotter than a hot text –

(LIZZIE *is now panting happily,* KAREN *laughs.)*

We do this to each other like every other day – the best was when I was in a crowded elevator in Salt Lake City –

FRANCINE. Excuse me. Can we please just do this?

KAREN. Okay. Right. Sorry. I'm sorry.

LIZZIE. Can you forward me that message? I could use it tonight.

FRANCINE. What site should we be on, Karen?

KAREN. I'm thinking "DreamDresses.com"

(LIZZIE *and* FRANCINE *type.)*

LIZZIE. Oooo.

FRANCINE. Mm.

KAREN. They can ship in five-to-seven business days and if you order $2,000 or more, they include a dozen roses free of charge.

LIZZIE. That is so cool.

FRANCINE. For 5,000 do they include a divorce attorney?

KAREN. No, but they do pre-nuptials on their sister site "Impermanence.com"

LIZZIE. But you're not doing pre-nups are you?

KAREN. Do you think I should?

FRANCINE. So what dresses are we looking at?

KAREN. On the left hand side, click on "Sexy/Sassy"

FRANCINE. Done.

LIZZIE. Wow.

KAREN. Is it "wow"?

LIZZIE. Oh, Karen!

KAREN. I'm looking at "Shoulder Exposé" or "The Jaw Dropper."

LIZZIE. They're gorgeous!

FRANCINE. They're very nice…

LIZZIE. They're fun! They say "I'm getting married and I'm going to have sex very very soon!"

FRANCINE. Did you look at the "Sunshine Smile" – it's still fun but it says "I'm going to wait until I leave the church to have sex."

KAREN. I like that, too.

LIZZIE. I haven't seen you in a while, Karen, how big are your breasts?

KAREN. What?

LIZZIE. The "Daring Dive" looks nice, but it draws attention to places I don't know if you want to draw attention –

FRANCINE. You don't exactly have time to send it back if it's not good on you –

KAREN. No, but click on the "Bride to Be" bar and type "Karen 3340"

(**FRANCINE** and **LIZZIE** type. Pause.)

FRANCINE & LIZZIE. Oh my god!

FRANCINE. How did they get your head on the dress?

KAREN. I sent them a JPEG of my face and measurements – they attach it to any dress you click on now.

LIZZIE. There you are in "Mistress Midnight"! And "Silk Surrender"! And –

FRANCINE. You look great, Karen. Did you touch up this photo at all?

KAREN. No!

LIZZIE. Is there a place where I can do this with cars? I want to see my head in different cars to see how I like them –

FRANCINE. Karen, have you checked the "Classy Classics" section?

KAREN. I did –

FRANCINE. I'm always partial to more conservative dresses –

KAREN. I don't know, I wanted something fun.

FRANCINE. "Meadow Blossom" is nice – it diminishes your hips.

KAREN. Do you think so?

FRANCINE. "Classic 50's."…"Classic 40's" – these are nice…

KAREN. That's true…

FRANCINE. "Classic 30's" is close to what I wore on my wedding.

KAREN. I know.

FRANCINE. I think that's really lovely. All the guests thought so – I got more notes and e-mails for months afterward – 98% positive –

KAREN. But your figure is better than mine –

FRANCINE. You have a lovely figure.

KAREN. No, I don't –

FRANCINE. You do.

KAREN. It's not as perfect as yours –

FRANCINE. Lizzie, doesn't Karen have a completely fine figure?

LIZZIE. I made a hundred Karens in a hundred dresses! You could marry the entire Green Bay Packers!

FRANCINE. What I don't see are prices.

KAREN. They're totally reasonable –

FRANCINE. How do I get to prices?

KAREN. Let's just look at styles right now –

FRANCINE. I just want to know –

LIZZIE. You have to click on the hemline.

FRANCINE. *(clicks)* …oh.

KAREN. Francine –

FRANCINE. This dress is $4,000.

KAREN. Which is kind of steep compared with some of the others –

FRANCINE. I can't let you spend $4,000 on a dress.

KAREN. It's my credit card, Francine, you can't –

FRANCINE. Okay, look, I checked around a bit myself this morning and I found some really lovely dresses at "SensibleBride.com" and "RealisticExpectations.net" –

KAREN. I don't want Realistic, I want Dream Dresses! This is my wedding, Francine!

FRANCINE. And on your salary –

KAREN. How much was your dress?

FRANCINE. That's completely beside the point –

KAREN. Your's was like $3,000 or something, wasn't it?

FRANCINE. Thirty-three-hundred, but that was my wedding –

KAREN. So?

FRANCINE. That was a real wedding, Karen, a serious wedding.

(beat)

KAREN. What did you just say?

FRANCINE. There are different kinds of weddings, that's all, there are weddings you plan for 18 months and weddings you throw together in two weeks.

KAREN. I am not –

FRANCINE. You pay $4,000 for a dress for a grown-up wedding, Karen, not for a kid's make-believe.

KAREN. This is not make-believe –

FRANCINE. I'm sorry, this is some guy no one ever met, you've barely met – some internet ghost you've known for a few weeks and you're in "love" –

KAREN. And how did you meet Michael?

FRANCINE. Excuse me?

KAREN. Did you meet Michael face to face?

FRANCINE. Eventually. Yes.

KAREN. "Mate-a-Rama.com," Francine? You guys wrote back and forth for what, a year?

FRANCINE. Eight months.

KAREN. Because you had to get him to fall in love with who you pretended you were until he was in so deep that when he did meet you he couldn't run screaming like every other man you'd ever dated for more than a week –

FRANCINE. We were establishing a bond, laying a solid foundation for love –

KAREN. You knew once he met you, you'd have to get a ring out of him in the first few minutes or he'd be out of there –

FRANCINE. How dare you??

KAREN. Of course you're jealous of me! I found a guy who fell in love with me the first time he met me – actually *met* me, no preamble, no written seduction – standing at the continental breakfast buffet at the Sheraton – I finally did something better than you and you can't stand it!!

FRANCINE. Is there even a "Max Aphelion," Karen? Or is this your mid-life fever imagination just conjuring him up? One last pathetic attempt to play grown-up and sit at the big table – at least everyone's met my husband, talked to him, touched him! You want to play your sad little games you can do it without me!

(She slams her phone shut and storms off.)

*(Long pause. **LIZZIE** and **KAREN** sit there on their phones…)*

LIZZIE. …I found a nice dress for only $975.

*(**KAREN** hangs up and wheels off. **LIZZIE** sits a moment…)*

…Karen?

*(Her laptop beeps. She pushes a button as **MICHAEL** wheels on typing on his computer – we hear what he and **LIZZIE** type as a Voice-Over as they work silently.)*

MICHAEL. *(V.O.)* Lizzie. Just thought I'd see if you have any dirt on Mr. Mystery.

LIZZIE. *(V.O.)* *(typing)* I'm online now. Just off the phone shopping with Karen and Francine.

MICHAEL. *(V.O.)* How'd that go?

LIZZIE. *(V.O.)* You ever see photos of Hiroshima?

MICHAEL. *(V.O.)* Ouch.

LIZZIE. *(V.O.)* Where are you?

MICHAEL. *(V.O.)* Outside of Topeka. Staying off the phone so Francine can call. Thought I'd say "hi."

LIZZIE. *(V.O.)* Hi.

MICHAEL. *(V.O.)* I was pitching our package to this hotel chain and they walked me through their new wing and in this one room they were building a T.V. case and entertainment cabinet thing – so of course I thought of you.

LIZZIE. *(V.O.)* I remind you of an entertainment cabinet?

MICHAEL. *(V.O.)* When you were trying to build one in college. In your living room. And you called me over that night.

LIZZIE. *(V.O.)* Ah.

MICHAEL. *(V.O.)* It was so primal. You were laying on the rug in that sweatshirt and cut-offs and looked up when I walked in and just smiled –

LIZZIE. *(V.O.)* My hero.

MICHAEL. *(V.O.)* To kneel beside you on the floor – the only light from the streetlights outside –

LIZZIE. *(V.O.)* I like starting after the world is asleep.

MICHAEL. *(V.O.)* Acting totally on instinct, to find the right tool – I remember the Phillips caught the light –

LIZZIE. *(V.O.)* I remember guiding your hand –

MICHAEL. *(V.O.)* And pressing it into the screw you already had half-in –

LIZZIE & MICHAEL. *(V.O.)* – and turning…

MICHAEL. *(V.O.)* That gentle pressure, pushing, pushing, pushing –

LIZZIE. *(V.O.)* …til it was in tight.

MICHAEL. *(V.O.)* And then again and again….

LIZZIE. *(V.O.)* …and again and again…

MICHAEL. *(V.O.)* Working our way up the cabinet…

LIZZIE. *(V.O.)* …inch by inch…

MICHAEL. *(V.O.)* …holding the shelves as we went…

LIZZIE. *(V.O.)* One plunge at a time…

MICHAEL. *(V.O.)* …til everything was flushed and arched –

LIZZIE. *(V.O.)* Looking for another opening, the next move –

MICHAEL. *(V.O.)* Fitting piece after piece after piece –

LIZZIE. *(V.O.)* Shoving against the wall for support –

MICHAEL. *(V.O.)* Breathing together –

LIZZIE. *(V.O.)* Whispering in the dark –

MICHAEL. *(V.O.)* Oh god –

LIZZIE. *(V.O.)* Oh god –

(**MICHAEL**'s *phone rings.*)

MICHAEL. *(out loud)* Oh god!

(*He fumbles the phone to his ear, clicks it on –*)

LIZZIE. *(V.O.) (typing)* Michael?

(**FRANCINE** *enters on her phone with a clipboard.*)

FRANCINE. Michael!

MICHAEL. What?!

FRANCINE. Are you okay?

MICHAEL. Hey, Francine! I'm fine! Great! How are you??

FRANCINE. Have you been running? You sound out of breath?

MICHAEL. No, I'm just…in my hotel! Sitting here alone!

FRANCINE. …doing what?

LIZZIE. *(V.O.) (typing)* Michael, are you there?

MICHAEL. Running from the bathroom. I ran to the phone. What's up, babe?

FRANCINE. Nothing.

MICHAEL. You don't sound like "nothing."

LIZZIE. *(V.O.) (typing)* Michael, should I keep waiting or start checking other e-mails?

FRANCINE. It's nothing! I'm just on my way into the group and I was just trying to help Karen and she turned on me like a wolverine and now I'm not even going to the stupid wedding if there's even going to be a stupid wed-

ding and I don't even care except that I do and I want
her to be happy and I hate her and I am so so lucky to
have you in my life and how unfair is it that Karen can't
find a perfect match and I love you and I really love
you and I had to call and say it and I miss you a lot a lot
a lot right now and I had to call…that's all.

MICHAEL. That's not nothing.

LIZZIE. *(V.O.) (typing)* Michael, I'm going. It's been lovely
reminiscing with you. Peace.

(She rolls out.)

MICHAEL. *(V.O.) (typing)* …Wait!

FRANCINE. And now I have to go test Mayoral slogans on a
bunch of voters, I love you, bye!

(She walks out.)

MICHAEL. *(into phone)* Wait!

(He's alone.)

…Can't anybody just wait?

(Lights shift as he wheels out and **KAREN** *and* **WALLY**
*sit on his couch staring at his unseen T.V., sounds of
commercials play quietly.* **KAREN** *dejectedly eats from a
half-gallon of ice cream. Pause. They stare.)*

KAREN. *(blankly)* You can speed through the commercials,
you know.

WALLY. I don't mind waiting. I figure they spent months
of their lives and thousands of their dollars to tell me
about their stuff, I can give 'em thirty seconds.

KAREN. You are the perfect T.V. watcher, Dad.

WALLY. *(shrugs)* I do my bit.

(Pause. More commercial sounds.)

So you want to talk about it yet?

*(She holds up the ice cream in answer and keeps eating,
staring.)*

Okey-dokey.

(Pause. They watch.)

Cause you know I think you got a lovely figure, but
I remember your mother was terrified one peanut
butter cookie and her wedding dress was kaput, and I
can't help noticing you're packin' away that gallon –

KAREN. There's no dress for me to fit into, Dad.

WALLY. Oh honey, I'm sure there must be one that fits you –

KAREN. There's thousands that fit me. I'm just not buying
them.

WALLY. Ah. You're leasing?

KAREN. I'm not leasing, Dad!

WALLY. Well, help me out here! You come to my house and
wanta play twenty questions – I'm no good at this. I'm
an idiot, sweetheart. You gotta lay it right out for me.

KAREN. I don't even think there's going to be a wedding.

WALLY. Okay. That's good and clear. Thank you.

(Beat. Realization.)

There's not going to be any wedding??

KAREN. Will you please mute the T.V.?

WALLY. *(fumbling with the remote, muting the T.V.)* Did he back
out? Is he already married? I can't believe it – he had
such a good phone handshake!

KAREN. He's not married –

WALLY. Well, he sounded fine, but you can't actually see his
eyes, you know, you can't tell – like some of those love
songs on the radio, you can't tell if they're singing to a
girl or a Border Collie, you know –

KAREN. Max doesn't even know about it. I'm the one back-
ing out.

WALLY. So it's your choice?

KAREN. *(nods)* And it's probably a mistake. Like saying "yes" in
the first place was probably a mistake. Like every choice
I make is a mistake. Like my life has been a mistake –

WALLY. Whoa, whoa, whoa.

(takes the ice cream)

I'm doin' an intervention here. Nobody's whole *life* is
a mistake. Not even your uncle Lloyd, and my god in

heaven, did that man make some doozies. You remember those geese? You remember that machete school?

KAREN. Dad –

WALLY. I'm just saying I've known you since your first hour on earth, sweetheart, and you have yet to scale the true heights of whoppers.

KAREN. Okay. But the wedding –

WALLY. How do you know it's a mistake?

(beat)

KAREN. …Francine told me.

WALLY. Oh, now! That's – That is – we're talking Francine, Karen!

KAREN. But she's right!

WALLY. Well, she's a great girl, but –

KAREN. – and Stuart too and common sense and everything says I'm screwing up again –

WALLY. I'm gonna call her. I'm gonna call her and we'll get to the bottom of this –

KAREN. Dad, don't –

WALLY. I am not having my little girl screw up my other little girl's big day!

(He gestures to the T.V. as he fumbles with his land line phone and address book.)

Will you push the pause? Or stop or whatever – this could take a while –

(KAREN picks up the remote and pushes a button as her cell rings.)

KAREN. (into phone) Hello?

(Lights up on LIZZIE at her computer, on the phone.)

LIZZIE. Hi, Karen, it's Lizzie. How are you, pumpkin?

KAREN. I've been better.

LIZZIE. I know. It's so tough when your own sister accuses you of being a delusional liar. I mean, speaking from my own experience. Except it wasn't my sister, it was my first three boyfriends. And my shrink.

KAREN. Lizzie –

LIZZIE. – and the UPS guy. But I think he just hated life.

KAREN. But Francine's right, I don't know if I should go through with this –

LIZZIE. Has Max given you a ring yet?

KAREN. What?

LIZZIE. An engagement ring. You don't have to go through with it until you accept his engagement ring. Everyone knows that.

KAREN. I didn't know that –

LIZZIE. Oops, I've got another call – can you hang on? Just hang on one itty bitty sec –

(pushes button)

Hello?

(MICHAEL appears in a different area with his rolling suitcase, talking on his cell.) Stage rt. Freq

MICHAEL. Lizzie, it's Michael – I have to talk to you.

LIZZIE. Oh poop.

MICHAEL. What?

WALLY. *(holding up his address book)* I got seventeen numbers for Francine – any idea which I should call?

(KAREN looks.)

LIZZIE. I want to talk to you, but Karen's on the other line – I think she's kind of on a cliff.

MICHAEL. What??

LIZZIE. A metaphorical cliff. I think.

MICHAEL. I just want to tell you – our I-M this afternoon –

LIZZIE. It was nice.

MICHAEL. It's just – I haven't felt that way in a while –

LIZZIE. Cool. I need to check with Karen. Hang on.

(pushes button)

Karen, are you still there?

KAREN. Of course. Where else am I going to go except further into my bucket of ice cream –

LIZZIE. Oh, sweet potato, you shouldn't do that, not so close to your honeymoon!

WALLY. *(to* **KAREN***)* Which one are you pointing to? This one or this one?

LIZZIE. Is that Mr. Fiancé I hear??

KAREN. It's my dad. I'm at my dad's –

(to **WALLY***)*

This is her new cell. Try that.

LIZZIE. While you're helping him, I need to check on something – hang on!

(pushes a button)

Hi, Michael. You were saying?

MICHAEL. Just that I hadn't thought about building that entertainment center in forever and it reminded me of other times – like when you planted that flower box –

LIZZIE. That *was* nice…

MICHAEL. With the marigolds.

LIZZIE. Just the smell of the soil and your hair –

MICHAEL. …shoot. I'm, ah, I'm –

(He pushes a button on his cell and **FRANCINE** *enters into still yet another area in a bathrobe on her cell phone.)*

Hello?

FRANCINE. Hi, Honey. Where are you?

MICHAEL. I'm…in the airport. Hi, Francine.

LIZZIE. *(pushes a button)* Hi, Karie, I'm back.

FRANCINE & KAREN. You sound funny. Are you okay?

LIZZIE. I'm scrumptious.

MICHAEL. I'm good. What's up?

WALLY. *(to* **KAREN***)* It's ringing.

FRANCINE. I've already taken my Xanax and I'm still clawing, I need to talk to someone – Shoot. Hang on.

(pushes a button)

Hello?

WALLY. Francine, it's me. Your father.

FRANCINE. Oh my god! Dad! Are you okay?

WALLY. What? I'm fine –

FRANCINE. Oh thank god. Then why are you calling me?

MICHAEL. *(pushes a button, whispered)* Lizzie? Lizzie, are you there?

LIZZIE. *(to* **KAREN***)* Listen, why don't you check on your dad, I'll be right back –

(pushes a button)

So you were saying about the soil?

FRANCINE. Did the hemorrhoids check out okay?

WALLY. They're fine, listen –

FRANCINE. Did you get that new container I sent?

WALLY. What container?

FRANCINE. For your blood pressure pills. It talks to you.

WALLY. I haven't put the batteries in yet.

MICHAEL. *(to* **LIZZIE***)* I'm kind of in an airport – I can't go into the soil too much here.

LIZZIE. Why not? We're just talking about planting seeds in a garden –

MICHAEL. I need to get back – I have another call – hang on –

FRANCINE. Hang on, Dad –

FRANCINE, MICHAEL, LIZZIE. Hey, Michael/Francine/Karen?

FRANCINE, MICHAEL, KAREN. Who are you talking to?

MICHAEL & LIZZIE. No one!

FRANCINE. My dad –

WALLY. She put me on hold.

FRANCINE. He can't even put his own batteries in his own pill dispenser.

MICHAEL. Do you need to talk to him, 'cause I can hang up –

FRANCINE. I want to talk to you – I need to hear your voice.

WALLY. Next thing she'll be asking me to e-mail her!

MICHAEL & LIZZIE. What should we talk about?

KAREN. Shoot, hang on.

(*pushes button*)

Hello?

(*And* **STUART** *stumbles out into still yet another area, drunk, on his cell.*) *same place*

STUART. Karen, it's Stuart, we gotta talk.

KAREN. Oh god. Where are you?

STUART. I'm in Uganda, Karen! It's beautiful!

KAREN. That's great, I've got another call, can you hang on?

STUART. Story of my life, hang on for someone else's call…

KAREN. Have you been drinking?

STUART. Only since Tuesday.

LIZZIE. (*pushes button*) Michael, are you there?

FRANCINE. (*to* **MICHAEL**) When are we both due back home?

MICHAEL. I'll check my P̶a̶l̶m̶ ̶P̶i̶l̶o̶t̶ *Calendar* – hang on –

(*pushes button, whispers*)

Lizzie?

LIZZIE. Why are you whispering?

MICHAEL. (*punching his PDA, whispering*) I'm not whispering.

LIZZIE. Then I'm losing you.

WALLY. I think I lost her. I'm hangin' up.

KAREN. (*to* **WALLY**) Don't hang up.

STUART. (*to* **KAREN**) I'm not goin' anywhere 'til I've said what I have to say.

KAREN. I'm talking to my dad.

FRANCINE. (*pushes button*) Dad? Sorry to keep you waiting. Are you okay?

WALLY. Will you quit asking me if I'm okay?

WALLY, STUART, MICHAEL. I gotta tell you something.

FRANCINE, KAREN, LIZZIE. Actually can you hang on?

(*They all push their buttons.*)

KAREN. Lizzie.

FRANCINE. Michael?

LIZZIE. Karen?

KAREN, LIZZIE, FRANCINE. I'm back.

MICHAEL. *(quickly pushing his cell button, to* **FRANCINE***)* Hey, looks like I'm home Saturday. You?

FRANCINE. *(on her PDA)* Friday. I don't know if I can wait that long.

WALLY. *(to* **KAREN***)* Your wedding's gonna come and go before I can get off this phone!

KAREN. I don't even know if there's going to be a wedding.

LIZZIE. *(to* **KAREN***)* Then who does know?

WALLY. You wait 'til I talk to your sister – there's going to be a wedding.

MICHAEL. *(to* **FRANCINE***)* They're going to board my flight. Can I call you when I land in Montgomery?

FRANCINE. Just tell me you love me and I'm not a total screw-up.

KAREN, LIZZIE, MICHAEL. Can you hang on?

(All push buttons.)

Sorry, Stuart/Mikie/Lizzie –

STUART. I am standing in downtown Soroti wondering why I can hear your every word 6,400 miles away and yet I cannot whisper what's in my heart!

KAREN. What?

MICHAEL. *(whispered, to* **LIZZIE***)* I have to run, but there's something I have to tell you –

LIZZIE. Will you stop whispering?, I can barely hear you.

FRANCINE. *(pushing her button, to* **WALLY***)* My own husband won't talk to me, Daddy.

WALLY. Well, if you give any of us more than five seconds –

MICHAEL. *(pushing a button)* Francine?

STUART. It's about your wedding, Karen.

LIZZIE. *(pushing a button)* Karen?

MICHAEL. *(pushing a button)* Lizzie?

FRANCINE. *(pushing a button)* Michael?

MICHAEL. Dammit!

(pushes a button)

WALLY. Dammit.

KAREN. *(to STUART)* Dammit, there's not even going to be a wedding!

STUART. I'm in love with you, Karen!

MICHAEL. *(to FRANCINE)* I'm still in love with you, Lizzie!

(beat)

KAREN, FRANCINE, & STUART. What?

MICHAEL. Um. Lizzie?

FRANCINE. No. This is Francine. Your wife.

MICHAEL. Oh…crap.

(He pushes a button.)

KAREN & STUART. What did you just say?

STUART & KAREN. No, you first –

FRANCINE. *(to MICHAEL)* What did you just say??

(DING DONG. KAREN and WALLY look up.)

WALLY. Great. Someone's at the door.

(He walks off, stretching the looooong phone cord.)

MICHAEL. Lizzie?

LIZZIE. Michael?

MICHAEL. I think I just told my wife I loved you.

LIZZIE. Why would you do that?

MICHAEL. Dammit!

(punches his button)

Francine?

FRANCINE. Michael, what did you just tell me?

STUART. There's more I need to tell you, Karen.

KAREN. I need to hang up now, Stuart.

LIZZIE. Helloooo?

MICHAEL. *(to FRANCINE)* Listen, you weren't supposed to hear that –

FRANCINE. Obviously not.

MICHAEL. I was speaking to Lizzie metaphorically –

FRANCINE. Oh god.

STUART. Is there not going to be a wedding?

No! Yes! I don't know!

: 'Cause I gotta tell you, on my flight from Tashkent
Kampala –

:L. *(to FRANCINE)* My flight is leaving, I have to call
ı –

FRANCINE. You don't have to do anything. Nobody does.
What do I care, is anybody listening?

(WALLY re-enters with a Fed Ex box.)

WALLY. *(to KAREN)* It's a package for you.

KAREN. At your address?

STUART. *(to KAREN)* That's just it. I don't have an address,
I don't have anything real, I just want something real,
Karen –

LIZZIE. *(pushing buttons at random)* Michael? Karen? Michael?
Karen?

STUART. Oh, for God's sake! My battery's going!!

KAREN. *(opening the package)* Stuart, we shouldn't be talking
now, there's no wedding, there's no Uganda, there's
nothing, okay, there's just nothing –

MICHAEL. *(to FRANCINE)* There's nothing I can say?

FRANCINE. There's nothing you can do.

WALLY. *(to KAREN)* That's it, I'm giving up.

WALLY, FRANCINE, LIZZIE, & KAREN. Goodbye!

MICHAEL & STUART. …goodbye?

*(Lights out on all but WALLY and KAREN, who pulls a
little box from the package…)*

KAREN. It's from Rings-Of-Life.com…Max just Fed-Exed
me an engagement ring.

(Blackout)

End of Act I

ACT II

(Lights come up on KAREN, FRANCINE, *and* MICHAEL *facing us, making separate presentations.)*

KAREN. *(to Audience)* Good morning. It's great to be here. First let me just assure everyone that my presence here doesn't in any way at all indicate that anyone is about to be fired. Ha ha ha, no, no, no. I'm here for one reason and that's to help you. You are part of the Hometown Buffet family, and like any family, we want every member to succeed.

MICHAEL. *(to Audience)* So you're asking yourselves, "Why a specific insurance policy on the satellite dishes of all Ramada Inns? This is bound to cost more than just repairing or replacing any given glitch on any given dish as it comes up, right?" Sadly, wrong. Here's a startling fact: "43% of satellite dishes will malfunction within eighteen months of warranty expiration."

FRANCINE. *(to Audience)* 53% of you say you want underwear that is "comfortable and unobtrusive." 21% of you said you want underwear that makes a clear personal statement to the world. And 8% of you said it has to be cheap.

MICHAEL. If 43% of the dishes on your 1000-plus hotels were to fail at an average cost of $325 each to repair – that's $140,000! And that's only in 18 months!

KAREN. It's everything from the placement of your Norman Rockwell paintings to whether the sprinkles and cherries are sufficiently segregated on the dessert bar.

FRANCINE. In light of this, I would like to turn your attention to these.

(holds up a LARGE bright-colored pair of boxer shorts)

Do you all have your pencils and rating cards?

KAREN. Because, as in every facet of life there is a right way…and a wrong way to go about things…

MICHAEL. There are a lot, *a lot* of things that can go wrong.

FRANCINE. I'd like you to look at these and think of your spouse.

MICHAEL. There you are, just doing your job, cruising along, sending and receiving, and suddenly – BZZT. Short circuit.

KAREN. Because there must be a reason why traditions work, you know – just because some domineering person out to control your life chastises you for not following *her* right way doesn't mean it's *not* the right way.

FRANCINE. Ladies, you see your husband in these, do you think A: fun, silly, sexy. B: ridiculous, childish, grow up. Or C: …That fat tub of lard wouldn't know a good thing even after 6-1/2 years.

MICHAEL. Who's to say? Could be a design flaw, could be an act of nature – totally natural, totally normal, but suddenly everyone's screaming at you "How could you?" "I don't believe this!" "You selfish bastard" –

KAREN. It's all about paying attention – when you just blast along, think you're being an adult, WHOOSH, you're off, and that's when you lose a thumb slicing the ham! And then, well then you've ruined your thumb *and* the ham, that ham is now unservable!

MICHAEL. You've been standing at attention in the proper place at the proper time for 6-1/2 years, and one little foul-up and the world comes to an end!

FRANCINE. These Look comfortable, Look uncomfortable, Look like my cheating husband left 'em on my best friend's bedroom floor!

MICHAEL. And it's not like technically you've even *done* anything! You just *thought* about malfunctioning –

KAREN. Nobody's gonna want to eat that ham.

MICHAEL. And now you're being RIPPED off the roof and thrown in the scrap heap!

FRANCINE. *(grabbing the boxers)* Or do you take the contents of these shorts and just squeeeeeeeze and twist –

KAREN. That ham is now totally inedible.

MICHAEL. You just wanta look up to the sky and scream "I DIDN'T DO ANYTHING WRONG!"

FRANCINE. *(to shorts)* I'll give you fun fashion briefs!

(hurls them to the floor, stomping and stomping and stomping them)

THIS is fun! FUN! FUN! FUN! FUN!!

MICHAEL. *(overlapping, yelling at the sky)* You're not the boss of me! You are NOT the boss of me!! You are not!!

KAREN. *(overlapping)* You want to sit at the adult table, you keep your stupid fingers intact and get engaged more than a week before the wedding!

(Beat. They all realize where they are....pause.)

MICHAEL. Huh.

KAREN. Um.

FRANCINE. Yeah.

KAREN. I, ah...I need to freshen up.

MICHAEL. I just – I'll be right back.

FRANCINE. Sorry. That wasn't one of the choices. Don't mark that.

KAREN, MICHAEL, FRANCINE. Excuse me.

(And KAREN darts off as lights shift and MICHAEL and FRANCINE circle the stage, never exiting, but grabbing up their cell phones.)

FRANCINE. Hello.

MICHAEL. Francine it's Michael don't hang up!

FRANCINE. Oh god –

MICHAEL. Can you talk, I've gotta talk –

FRANCINE. Yeah, well, right now I have to go back into a group and try to save our Fruit of the Loom account –

MICHAEL. Can you come up with an excuse for me too, while you're at it? 'Cause I just screamed at the entire Ramada Inn Purchasing Department, when I should have been explaining to you –

FRANCINE. I don't want an explanation. I want it gone.

MICHAEL. What?

FRANCINE. I want it to never have happened. I want that to be the kind of thing that happens to other people, not to you. Not to me.

MICHAEL. Me too! I'm totally good with that. Let's say it never happened –

FRANCINE. We can't pretend, Michael.

MICHAEL. No, no pretending, we're not pretending, we're facing the facts and dealing with it. And the fact I'm dealing with is that nothing happened.

FRANCINE. How can you say that?

MICHAEL. Because it's the truth. I said a stupid thing –

FRANCINE. You said you loved her.

MICHAEL. Yes, "said," not "do," "said." Very different verbs.

FRANCINE. Do you make a habit of telling people you love them when you don't?

MICHAEL. Absolutely!

FRANCINE. Oh god.

MICHAEL. But not you! When I say I love you, I do love you, not "say" but "do"! Say *and* do! I do so I say!

FRANCINE. Michael –

MICHAEL. I *say* I'm gonna kill that guy in Nebraska who filed the false claims with us and won, but do I kill him? I may take a pile of dog crap and smear it all over his dish before I leave for the airport, but do I kill him?

FRANCINE. You do *what*?

MICHAEL. My point is I say a lot of stuff. I say "I love you" to clients all the time – I give 'em hugs, a kiss on the cheek, a pat on the ass –

FRANCINE. What?

MICHAEL. But I don't *love* them! Do you see my point?

FRANCINE. How many clients do you "pat on the ass"?

MICHAEL. Not that many, some, a few, you're missing my point!

FRANCINE. You're not helping yourself here –

MICHAEL. I'm being honest with you! I'm showing you my honesty. And my honesty is that I love you and only you. Would I be melting down in a sales pitch if I didn't?

FRANCINE. You'd be melting down because you know I'm due back home before you and I could change the locks.

MICHAEL. Would you do that?

FRANCINE. I don't know –

MICHAEL. Well, because then I'd just, I could sue you. And I'd get half the house – easy, half the house – so you'd be crazy to piss me off –

FRANCINE. Are you threatening me?

MICHAEL. I'm apologizing! I'm apologizing with a big stick. It's a win/win or a lose/lose, Francine, for both of us! Let's make it a win/win!

FRANCINE. I don't believe this.

MICHAEL. Well, neither do I. I say one stupid thing – a stupid thing that wasn't even *to* you – you were practically eavesdropping –

FRANCINE. You were talking to me on the phone –

MICHAEL. And now you're threatening to change the locks because of what you think you maybe heard and misunderstood and that's a hell of a way to say thank you, Francine!

FRANCINE. "Thank you"?

MICHAEL. For marrying you in the first place. For sticking with you all this time.

FRANCINE. What?

MICHAEL. You're not the most ant-free picnic, you know.

FRANCINE. I never said I was ant-free –

MICHAEL. I gotta come up for air every once in a while, Francine, it's pretty petty to be dragging me back under just because you don't want to breathe –

FRANCINE. I breathe, Michael, I breathe too –

MICHAEL. Then come up for air with me! Don't be an anchor, Francie, be a noodle!

FRANCINE. What?

MICHAEL. One of those long Styrofoam noodles the kids swim with – buoy me up sometimes, Francine.

FRANCINE. Have I been an anchor?

MICHAEL. Couldn't you hear me gasping for air?

FRANCINE. I never heard you gasping.

MICHAEL. You gotta listen. A marriage is about listening, Francine.

FRANCINE. I try to listen –

MICHAEL. Then you gotta try harder.

FRANCINE. …I'm sorry.

MICHAEL. We gotta be each other's noodles, Francine. Are you gonna be my noodle or not?

FRANCINE. …I'll try. I thought I was trying.

MICHAEL. We both gotta try harder. And I gotta try to save my job – we're out of the water and back on solid ground, right?

FRANCINE. I'm not –

MICHAEL. Don't go back in, Francine. Don't go there.

FRANCINE. I don't think –

MICHAEL. Think love. Think noodles. I'll call you. Bye-bye.

(*They hang up…*FRANCINE *pauses…then hurries off.* MICHAEL *starts out – his phone rings – he answers as* LIZZIE *enters on her phone, eating microwave popcorn from a bag.*)

Hello?

LIZZIE. Michael, it's Lizzy, don't hang up.

(MICHAEL *winces.*)

MICHAEL. Actually, this is a bad bad bad –

LIZZIE. I want to talk about you loving me.

MICHAEL. …yeah. Okay, absolutely, I've really gotta run, but what you need to know is that Francine and I have been having some problems, that's all – or she's been

having problems, I'm having problems with her problems, and part of her problems is that she didn't even
know I was having problems.

LIZZIE. That's a problem.

MICHAEL. But I think we've kind of fixed it. So maybe
it's okay, sometimes, you and me just talking. Or…
"talking."

LIZZIE. What about you still loving me?

MICHAEL. Well. You know. That's, I mean, I don't know if
that's part of the talking. Or "talking."

LIZZIE. But is it part of the feeling? Or "feeling"?

MICHAEL. …do you want it to be?

LIZZIE. Well, if you're gonna say it, sure. Otherwise you
might as well say "I'm repulsed by carrot cake." You
know?

MICHAEL. I'm not sure what you're saying.

LIZZIE. Are you repulsed by carrot cake or not?

MICHAEL. …no.

LIZZIE. Then why say you are?

MICHAEL. I didn't.

LIZZIE. Exactly.

(beat)

MICHAEL. Lizzie, listen, I desperately need to go to a
meeting –

LIZZIE. Do you want to get back together with me?

MICHAEL. No! I mean not like – I don't– Mostly I'm just
trying to go to a meeting –

LIZZIE. So the meeting is more important than us?

MICHAEL. Is there an us?

LIZZIE. I don't think so.

MICHAEL. Then the meeting's more important.

LIZZIE. Was there ever an us, do you think, Michael? I mean
there was a you and me, absolutely, but the whole "us"
thing, you know.

MICHAEL. There was an "us," absolutely.

LIZZIE. And now there's still a you and me…and there's this "non-us" too. Isn't that odd?

MICHAEL. I'm gonna call you later, okay?

LIZZIE. But you're going to be calling Francine later too, right?

MICHAEL. Not at the same time, not again, never again. I've just got to sort through my feelings –

LIZZIE. *(siren-like)* Ah-Wooga! Ah-Wooga! Danger, Will Robinson, Danger!

MICHAEL. Lizzie –

LIZZIE. I spend every waking moment of my life sorting through my feelings. I want to talk to someone who *knows* what he feels so I can figure out how I feel about his feelings. If everyone's sorting, my god, it's like wheat threshing in Hell.

MICHAEL. Lizzie –

LIZZIE. I mean, I've never threshed wheat anywhere, but I can imagine –

MICHAEL. I want to stay in touch, Lizzie –

LIZZIE. Me too.

MICHAEL. So I'll call you –

LIZZIE. And I won't answer.

MICHAEL. Lizzie!

LIZZIE. I've never seen an MRI of you, Michael.

MICHAEL. What??

LIZZIE. I have no idea how big your heart is. You may have such a super large heart that there's enough love in there for 23 women equally. But I've seen your head. And your skull is the same size as everyone else's. Which means that your brain is the same size as everyone else's, which means you've only got the same amount of attention, no matter how much love you've got. And any attention I take up is attention Francine's not getting, and right now she needs the attention because there is an "us" there – you and her – I've seen it. It may be sputtering, clanging, I-can't-feel-my-fingers right now, but there is an "us" there. And you take an "us" over a "non-us" any minute of the day. So you should call her, and I hope she answers. But if you call me, I won't.

MICHAEL. Lizzie, please –

LIZZIE. No.

MICHAEL. Can I –

LIZZIE. No.

MICHAEL. Please!

LIZZIE. No.

(She hangs up and redials as **MICHAEL** *slunks off.)*

*(***KAREN** *enters with her phone, shouting Off-stage.)*

KAREN. No, I was kidding about the ham and finger thing, it was, it was a metaphor, I love pork products –

(answers her cell)

Hello!

LIZZIE. How are you, Nuptial Girl?

KAREN. *(quietly)* I've died and gone to Hell in Reno. There aren't going to be any nuptials.

LIZZIE. I knew it! He's already married, isn't he? I can't believe this! Two married men in one day! What is it, like the flu?

KAREN. He's not married.

LIZZIE. Oh.

KAREN. What are you talking about? What married men?

LIZZIE. …nothing.

KAREN. He sent me an engagement ring.

LIZZIE. Well, that's it then.

KAREN. Lizzie.

LIZZIE. Is it a nice ring?

KAREN. I haven't taken it out of the box.

LIZZIE. Is it a nice box?

KAREN. It's a lovely box.

LIZZIE. Well, that's it then.

KAREN. One ring –

LIZZIE. – means he's serious! You should be grateful! You know how many men shuffle and mutter? They glance at you out of the corner of their eye, never look at you full on, too busy "sorting out feelings" and talking and "talking" to step up and say "Yes. This is what I feel and you are the one I feel it for."

KAREN. But what if I don't feel it for him?

LIZZIE. Oh, you do not get to tell me you're "sorting out your feelings."

KAREN. I kind of am, yeah.

LIZZIE. NO! No no no! You loved him yesterday.

KAREN. Yes –

LIZZIE. And all he's done since then is say he loves you by giving you a lovely box.

KAREN. But what if I'm just scared of not having anyone? How do you tell the difference between love and desperation?

LIZZIE. Is there a difference?

KAREN. I should take more time, that's all, I should send back the ring and demand more time – I mean I'm bound to be more mature in 35, 40 years, aren't I?

LIZZIE. I had this friend – have – she's still with us, or was as of last Wednesday – her name's Maureen and she got married right out of high school, met this guy – Terrance – in her Psych 101 class freshman year and BAM. No question, no sorting out feelings, Cupid took aim, Whoosh-Thunk, and they got married. Best thing she ever did.

KAREN. How long have they been married?

LIZZIE. They got divorced by her senior year.

KAREN. Oh god.

LIZZIE. But she lived more in her sophomore and junior years than most people do in a lifetime!

KAREN. I don't think –

LIZZIE. Ooh! Or Salina Tolliver! She met Ricky on-line – he was in Lisbon and she was in Baton Rouge! They hardly ever met face to face, they were on the road constantly, but it was love, true love – they planned their wedding long distance and it was beautiful. The photos are on their website!

KAREN. And when did they get divorced?

LIZZIE. They didn't.

KAREN. Oh.

LIZZIE. But…Ricky kind of died in a plane crash in southern France. It was a business trip.

KAREN. Oh jesus.

LIZZIE. But the point is they were in love when he died.

KAREN. Do you have any stories where the couple is still together? Here on Earth? *(pause)* Lizzie?

LIZZIE. I'm thinking.

KAREN. Oh man.

LIZZIE. Isn't that odd? I must know someone who's still happily married…

KAREN. Besides Francine and Michael.

(**LIZZIE** *scoffs.*)

What?

LIZZIE. *(coughing)* Nothing. Nothing.

KAREN. *(looks at her phone)* That'll be Max on the other line.

LIZZIE. Cool beans. I'll check back later.

KAREN. I'm not answering it.

LIZZIE. What?

KAREN. He's called and texted five times since he sent the ring, and I haven't answered.

LIZZIE. Why?

KAREN. I don't know what to say!

LIZZIE. Tell him it's a lovely box!

KAREN. I'll end up crying and telling him I don't know what to do and I don't even have a dress and I don't have invitations and I don't have a minister because I haven't even stepped in a church outside an airport chapel in three years – if I get married now, God's gonna look down and go "Who?"

LIZZIE. I'll be your minister.

KAREN. What?

LIZZIE. I got ordained on-line last year. I can be your minister. I've got a terrific vest and hat! I'll drive up, we'll do it at your house, just friends and you and your dad, we'll convince him to turn off the T.V. for the ceremony –

KAREN. I'm glad you're so enthused –

LIZZIE. This is love, Karen! If it's bothered to walk in your door you've gotta tackle it, knock it to the carpet and pin it and pull a couch over on top of it –

KAREN. And how do you know?

LIZZIE. What?

KAREN. What makes you the big expert on love, Lizzie? How many relationships have you had that lasted more than a week? I love you, but I'm not gonna take advice on a lifetime decision from a woman who can't decide what color eyes she's gonna have today!

LIZZIE. They're brown. I did decide. I went with brown. So can I officiate? It'll be a blast, I'm legal –

KAREN. No.

LIZZIE. Can I –

KAREN. No!

LIZZIE. Please!

KAREN. No!

(And **KAREN** *hangs up and walks out.* **LIZZIE** *pauses, then stalks out with her popcorn bag.)*

(Lights shift and **MICHAEL** *and* **STUART** *enter in two separate areas on the phone.* **MICHAEL** *has a bottle of beer in his hand,* **STUART** *with an ornate wine glass in his. They are both drunk.)*

MICHAEL. No!

STUART. No!

MICHAEL. Where? Where's the big book where it says they can treat us like this?

STUART. Nowhere! I've never seen such a book!

MICHAEL. A brochure? A pamphlet?

STUART. Nothing. In fact, I'm pretty sure in the one big book it says women are property of men! Chattel!

MICHAEL. I like that book. I vote we go back to that book.

STUART. Of course, I think it also says we have to forgive the people who piss us off –

MICHAEL. Let's go back to the chattel part. I like the chattel part.

STUART. I mean, not that I'd be a particularly good master. I had these, these sea-monkeys I got for my birthday and within a month their little jar was caked with algae and they were eating each other and digging through the calcified corpses of their brethren for any hint of oxygen…but I think I'd make a pretty good husband.

MICHAEL. You'd make a fantastic husband.

STUART. As long as I wasn't in charge of food and air and cleaning her cage, I'd be okay I think.

MICHAEL. But see, they don't want a benign master. They want a subject. They want chattel of their own.

STUART. …I'd be okay with that. As long as they clean my cage and feed me, I'm good.

MICHAEL. That's why you're not married. They can smell it on you. You're willing to be a subject.

STUART. But that's what they want?

MICHAEL. No, see, they want you to bite at the cage, to put up a fight and jump around and throw feces at the glass, but…BUT at the end of the day you'll still cuddle up and go to sleep in your little room.

STUART. So…I have to be a *grouchy* tame monkey?

MICHAEL. Yes. Women want grouchy tame monkeys. That is how you get a mate.

(Pause. They drink.)

STUART. I wonder if Karen likes monkeys.

MICHAEL. All women like monkeys. And as long as we were out on the field, in the savannah grasslands, that's fine, but when we let'em start building houses – when they realized they could keep their monkeys indoors –

STUART. That was the slippery slope.

MICHAEL. We gotta demolish the zoos. We gotta get back onto the prairie where we can run free and yell "Come On!" and they come. 'Cause if they don't – we got other younger females will be happy to follow us!

STUART. See, I never had that. I'd yell "Come On" and watch them happily scamper over to hairier monkeys. Maybe it's my scent. Maybe I smell like an evolutionary dead-end.

MICHAEL. Nomads. If we're gonna save the human race we gotta become nomads again. It's stasis that kills the species.

STUART. What are you drinking?

MICHAEL. Guiness Stout. You?

STUART. A local wine made in local Tangier.

MICHAEL. Do they need satellite dish insurance in Tangier?

STUART. ...I do not even know who to ask.

MICHAEL. You know what else kills species? Traps.

STUART. Certainly has been hard on the elephants, I'll tell you.

MICHAEL. I mean people traps. Gotcha traps. And you know who sets great goddam traps?

STUART & MICHAEL. Women!

(They drink.)

MICHAEL. It's all "be honest" and "we have to talk freely" and "tell me what you're feeling" and so you say "well, I love another woman" and SLAM-O!

STUART. Trap! Avoid the trap! Trap!

MICHAEL. Gnaw your own leg off to escape.

STUART. Or. OR you open your heart, pull the ribcage open – CRACK-AK-AK, say "Here I am, every throbbing oozing dribbling thing in here is yours!."...And they get married to someone else!

MICHAEL. ...I don't know if that's a trap exactly.

STUART. Well…it's not….

MICHAEL. Unless she led you on…

STUART. Not really.

MICHAEL. And honestly, I don't know how appealing the throbbing oozing stuff is, to be honest.

STUART. It's not. Not in the least.

MICHAEL. So, I mean, that's different.

STUART. But it hurts like a bear trap!

MICHAEL. Absolutely! Snap!

STUART. SNAP! OW!

MICHAEL. Ow!

STUART. No more ow's! I'm calling Karen right now –

MICHAEL. And I'm callin' my wife!

STUART. Because there is nothing – NOTHING – that tells a woman you're serious like a drunken phone call at 2:30 in the morning.

(beat)

MICHAEL. …Maybe we should wait.

STUART. Yes. No! I am going there! I am coming home and I am marching up face to face to her house or her father's house or wherever the hell she is Sunday and I am looking her and Max Stupid Aphelion in the eyes and I am Sharing My Feelings!!

MICHAEL. I am so there, compadre! I am standing by your side and if Francine wants the truth, she gets the truth!

STUART. In her face! I am reserving a plane ticket! Now!

MICHAEL. Yes!

STUART. Yes!

MICHAEL. YES!

STUART. YEAAHHHHH!!!

(They exit as lights shift and **FRANCINE** and **KAREN** wheel on in separate areas, prepping for work, each with her laptop.)

FRANCINE & KAREN. (calling out) I'll be there in a minute!

KAREN. Set out the syrup and french toast stix –

FRANCINE. Get'em all in the room looking at the photos of the can and bottle.

FRANCINE & KAREN. I just need to check this…

(They look at their screens as **WALLY** *wheels on between them, trying to type on his desktop computer while reading a sheet of handwritten instructions.)*

WALLY. *(typing and speaking)* Dear Karen and Francine. It's me. Your pop. To tell you Hell has frozen over. I'm e-mailing. I'm thinking this is my last chance to finish a thought without you putting me on hold or cutting me off or making me disappear. I now wish I'd taken typing in high school as it's taken me damn near 20 minutes to write the last five sentences. But in my day boys didn't type and girls didn't take shop. I bet there is a 65 year old woman out there trying to make an end table and losing fingers even as I type and there you go, the education system of 1956. I went to Ruth N. Bond Elementary School. It's not there anymore. There's a parking lot. But when I was there I hung out with Benton Shane, Sean Breckenridge, and Mel Tolbert and a few dozen other kids among whom was a girl. She had a pixie haircut and wore blue dresses and knocked Sean Breckenridge's tooth out on the teeter-totter one time. That's really all I remember about her. She was one of the faces I saw Monday through Friday week after week, month after month, for twelve years, just like everyone else I started school with. We knew each other inside and out, who cried easy, whose parents were drunks, who told the good dirty jokes, who would laugh til they peed their pants. We watched each other grow up without realizing that's what we were doing. And out of that stagnant pool of Hoover High School, which isn't there anymore, it's a Sam's Club – one day I looked over in gym class at the pixie cut girl, the same one I'd spent the previous twelve years watching grow up without paying any attention, and there she was laughing with a bunch of girls in the corner and I thought…"huh." That was it. No stars, no music, no angels. She didn't even look at me. I just thought "huh." And that "huh" changed my life. And hers. And yours. It didn't even lead to love, it led to a few smiles and an awkward conversation about the availability of ketchup at the concession stand. Anyone looking at us wouldn't have been able to say "Those kids will spend the next 43 years together and raise two incredible girls." Some people you could see it on the outside. Not us. The "huh" happens in here – all the Bentons and Seans and Mels in the world can't tell you when it's real or not or whether it'll last or not or whether it's worth it or not, and neither can I. All I can tell you is if you feel a "huh," keep your eye on that person. Smile a little more often. Even if you keep learning things about'em and it ticks you off, if they make lousy mistakes or you make lousy mistakes or you can barely remember the "huh" at all. If it's still there – even just the glowing head of the match after the fire's out – keep paying attention. 'Cause you may only have one day with them. Or a week. Or 43 years. But when it's over it won't have been enough. So say "huh" when you can. I'm gonna send this now. I hope. It's taken me two hours to write it and now I'm gonna put it in its bottle and throw it into the ocean of electricity. Damned if I even know where either of you are. But I love both of you more than you'll ever know. I'm going to bed. Dad.

(*He walks off.* **KAREN** *and* **FRANCINE** *stare at their screens…* **KAREN** *reaches into her purse and takes out the engagement ring box…looks at it…and opens it. She takes the ring out…and gently slides it on to her finger. Picks up her phone and dials.* **LIZZIE** *enters.*)

LIZZIE. Hello?

KAREN. (*into phone*) Lizzie, the wedding's on, I'd love for you to officiate, I'll call you right back.

(*She hangs up and re-dials quickly.*)

LIZZIE. Yes!

(*She charges off.*)

FRANCINE. Hello?

KAREN. Francine, the wedding's on, I'm ordering the dress I want because I've had a "huh" moment and I'm still having the "huh" and you can be part of it or not, I love you.

(She hangs up and re-dials.)

FRANCINE. …Karen?

KAREN. *(into phone)* Max? Hey, sweetheart…I know, I'm sorry, I didn't mean to scare you. I got your ring. It's beautiful…

(She exits as **FRANCINE** *dials and* **MICHAEL** *enters on his phone.)*

MICHAEL. Hey, Francie –

FRANCINE. Michael, listen, we need to talk, and by talk I mean be with each other, actually in the room "be with each other," because I'm tired of being in a hotel room that looks just like your hotel room in a city that looks just like your city talking on a phone that looks just like your phone. I want to talk without roaming charges or losing your signal or leaving in time to get through airport security. I want to *talk*. I'll be at my father's house at 4 p.m. Sunday for Karen's wedding and I'm ready to talk about noodles and breathing and you can be part of that discussion or not.

(She hangs up and walks out.)

MICHAEL. …Francine?

(DING DONG! A doorbell ring as **MICHAEL** *exits and* **WALLY** *enters in a nice suit setting out vases of flowers on either end of his couch. Lights shift. DING DONG again.)*

WALLY. I'm coming. I'm coming!

(calling off)

Karen, I think the main man himself is here!

(He steps offstage and in steps **STUART** *in a very sharp suit, walking very confidently and directly.)*

STUART. Hello, Mr. Baedeker. I need to speak to Karen!

WALLY. *(re-enters behind him)* Yeah, well, you need to speak to me first!

STUART. I'm sorry –

WALLY. She said you were impulsive!

STUART. She did?

WALLY. You just DO things. Like barging in demanding to see her, I suppose.

STUART. I'm sorry. I don't usually barge. Much more likely to inch or meander actually –

WALLY. Well, stop moving and gimme a second to look at you in the eye, young man.

(Beat. STUART stands uncomfortably.)

You're bigger than you look on the phone. I'm her father. Wally Baedeker.

STUART. I know. Sir.

(They shake.)

WALLY. Hm. You got a real different phone handshake too.

STUART. Excuse me?

WALLY. You can stop your worrying. She's here. Still changing. Unless she went out the window. And most of them don't open so good.

STUART. Right.

WALLY. So I can't really let you barge in on her.

STUART. Of course not. *(beat)* I may have done all my barging for the day anyway.

(beat)

WALLY. You want to sit down?

(STUART does. Pause.)

You want something to drink?

STUART. Dear God yes.

(Ding Dong from the door. STUART leaps up. WALLY heads off.)

WALLY. Another doorbell, another barger!

(He's gone. **STUART** *starts to remove his jacket, clears his throat, flexes his fists, clears his throat –)*

STUART. *(quickly to himself)* Mr. Aphelion, I believe you and I need to step outside. Sir, you and I need to talk outside. Mr. Aphelion –

(He spins to face **MICHAEL,** *entering quickly in a tasteful conservative suit.)*

SIR, YOU AND I ARE STEPPING OUT!

MICHAEL. Not now, Stuart. Where's Francine?

*(***WALLY** *walks in behind them.)*

WALLY. Not here yet. I thought you'd come together.

MICHAEL. Yeah, well, that's the question d'jour, isn't it?

(briskly shaking **STUART**'*s hand)*

You look good, man. World travel agrees with you.

STUART. Right back at you.

WALLY. *(to* **MICHAEL***)* You already met the big guy here?

MICHAEL. Sure.

WALLY. Probably through I-T or whatever, right? Phone pictures, right? I'm the last person on Earth who doesn't think he's met someone 'til we're in the same room.

*(***MICHAEL** *sits.* **STUART** *sits.* **WALLY** *waits. Pause…)*

WALLY. *(continued) (gestures to the vases beside the couch)* Been years since we had flowers in this house. *(beat)* I mean besides on the shower curtains. *(beat)* And the pot holders and the tile in the kitchen.*(beat)* And that wallpaper in the guest room. Come to think of it, I'm up to my eyeballs in flowers around here.

STUART. My strongest memory of flowers was this family trip we took when I was eight, out to visit my aunt in Vermont. And as we drove we passed this field. I mean a huge field, acres and acres of wildflowers, and not just one kind of wildflower, you know where one species pretty much commits flower genocide and wipes out every competing flower, no, there were dozens, two dozen, three dozen kinds of flowers – every color, every shape as far as the eye could see. And my father pulled over. Which was something considering we usually got one bathroom break per state – which gave us a keen sense of geography, let me tell you – Kansas is a very, very wide state it turns out – but we all just got out of the car – wordlessly, which was also something of first in my clan, and we just stood there staring at this ocean of color and texture.

MICHAEL. Wow.

STUART. Unfortunately, my mother insisted we go lie down in the flowers so she could get a picture, and we did, and it turns out not only was this a magical place for us, but was the single greatest magnet for honey bees in the tri-state region. We arrived at my aunt's house approximately three times the size we left our house.

WALLY. Holy cow.

STUART. So I have mixed feelings about flowers.

WALLY. Okay.

(He starts to carry them out.)

STUART. But these are lovely! These should stay!

WALLY. Okay.

(He sets them back down.)

WALLY. *(continued) (to* MICHAEL*)* Impulsive. That's what Karen calls it.

(Ding Dong. Doorbell. STUART *and* MICHAEL *leap up.)*

Sit down! Jesus, how much coffee do they give you on airplanes these days?

(He heads out as MICHAEL *and* STUART *brace for a fight with whoever walks through that door.)*

STUART. *(quickly to himself)* Mr. Aphelion, I think you and I need to step outside. Mr. Aphelion, I'm afraid you and I –

MICHAEL. What the hell are you talking about?

*(**LIZZIE** comes racing in wearing a wildly colorful funky outfit and floppy hat. She almost leaps on **STUART**.)*

STUART. SIR, OUTSIDE IS WHERE WE'RE STEPPING –

LIZZIE. Stuart!

STUART. ...Lizzie! Wow, Sorry, thought you were, I thought –

LIZZIE. You look fantastic! I haven't seen you since Francie's wedding!

*(to the entering **WALLY**)*

Doesn't he look dreamy – couldn't you just lick the cream out of his Oreo right here?

WALLY. I, ah, uh, ah –

LIZZIE. And you look super too, Mr. Baedeker. Very dignified, very patriarchal. In the best way.

WALLY. Thank you. You look... ah, clown-like...

STUART. In the best way. Very...cream-licking, as well.

LIZZIE. I thought it should be fun – don't you think this is fun?

WALLY. *(to **LIZZIE**)* I suppose you've already met the special fella here before too?

LIZZIE. I think we almost lived in the same city once.

WALLY. Hell, you're practically related.

LIZZIE. Well, we kind of are, aren't we?

*(**STUART** blanches a little.)*

Evolutionarily, right? I mean, this whole getting married thing is really kind of one gigantic state-sanctioned inbreeding party if you think about it. What an incestuous species we are –

WALLY. *(offering his hand to her)* I'm Wally Baedeker. I think you should stop talking about that now.

LIZZIE. Cool beans. I'm Lizzie Monahan. Distant relative.

*(turns to **MICHAEL**)*

And speaking of incest, Hello, Michael.

(She offers her hand.)

MICHAEL. Lizzie.

LIZZIE. You look very dashing as well. And Francine's here, right? You did come with Francine?

WALLY. Not yet.

(She steps away from **MICHAEL.***)*

LIZZIE. Ah.

MICHAEL. But she's coming. We're going to be here together.

(Ding Dong.)

WALLY. Maybe that's her now.

*(***STUART** *and* **MICHAEL** *brace, ready to go back into defense –)*

LIZZIE. *(to* **STUART***)* I mean it, you look positively page-turning. Doesn't he, Michael?

STUART. Thank you.

LIZZIE. I'm so used to thinking of you as the dweeby guy in Bunghole, Saudi Arabia. I have to totally realign my opinion.

STUART. Thank you.

(And **FRANCINE** *walks in wearing a very tasteful conservative outfit.* **STUART** *spins to face her –)*

STUART. *(continued)* SIR, IF YOU – oh for god's sake.

LIZZIE. Francie!

(She practically leaps on the startled **FRANCINE,** *holding her tight.)*

FRANCINE. Lizzie!

LIZZIE. *(to* **FRANCINE***)* Oh my god, you look so handsome, you could totally be a First Lady – probably a Republican First Lady –

FRANCINE. Stuart. You look very nice.

LIZZIE. I know! Can't you just see him as the new James Bond? But more sweaty?

*(***WALLY** *enters behind them.)*

FRANCINE. How are you, Dad?

WALLY. Pretty good, sweetheart. You look beautiful.

FRANCINE. Driving is still okay? You still feel safe behind the wheel?

WALLY. I figure that's what the horn is for, to get everybody out of the way.

FRANCINE. If it ever gets uncomfortable just tell us. We'll work something out. Karen can maybe drive you around. The house looks fine.

WALLY. I keep the dead cats and jars of my own urine down in the basement. Out of sight.

(She gives him a look. He smiles sweetly at her. She turns to face the waiting MICHAEL. They stare at each other. Beat.)

MICHAEL. Francine.

FRANCINE. Michael.

(Beat. Everyone gets it.)

WALLY. I should make some punch.

STUART. I'll join you.

LIZZIE. I love punch.

(They're gone. Beat. Awkward beat. MICHAEL holds up a little paper bag.)

FRANCINE. What.

(He gestures for her to take it. She does. Looks in it. Reacts.)

Is this…?

MICHAEL. Yeah. From Lulu's. I had a quick transfer in Phoenix. White Macadamia and peanut butter.

FRANCINE. …It's still soft.

MICHAEL. Is it still intact? I kept it in my CD case in my carry-on so it wouldn't get crushed –

FRANCINE. It's still intact.

MICHAEL. 'Cause I know how you like your cookies whole. Round. You know.

FRANCINE. Did you at least get one for yourself?

(He slowly pulls out another little paper bag.)

Chocolate chip caramel?

(He nods.)

MICHAEL. Can we try?

FRANCINE. The thing?

*(**MICHAEL** nods. She hesitates. Hands him her cookie. He hands her his. They watch each other, almost a smile…and offer each other the cookies.)*

MICHAEL. Um.

FRANCINE. Oh, right.

(She breaks off a piece of his and feeds it to him as he gives her a bite of hers, intact. Beat.)

MICHAEL. Your eyes look tired.

FRANCINE. So do yours. *(quietly)* So where do we stand on the whole "love" thing?

MICHAEL. Yeah.

FRANCINE. And I need to preface that by saying I may very well not believe a word that comes out of your mouth.

MICHAEL. Yeah.

FRANCINE. Because clearly on some level I don't know you, we're starting from scratch, or less than scratch, because what I do know is that you're the kind of man who leads a double life, where he's a great husband and friend and also smears dog crap and pats asses and tells other women that he loves them and god knows what else, and if there's one thing I know about double lives it's that at *least* one party is getting lied to and I am *not* going to be that party ever again, Michael, even if I haven't been the best noodle or picnic or whatever else, I *will not* be lied to. I can't.

MICHAEL. Okay, first the double life – it's not double, it's not half – the part you don't know about is like one-sixth, one-eighth of my life. So a good 85-90% of me is totally on the table for you. What you see is what you get.

FRANCINE. Okay.

MICHAEL. And that 10-15%, that part of me you wouldn't like. *I* don't like it, so there's way I'm gonna show it to one of the only people on earth who can stand me.

FRANCINE. How do you know I won't like it?

MICHAEL. Because when I mentioned the patting and dog –

FRANCINE. Okay. You're right. I don't like it.

MICHAEL. Exactly. And I don't want to lose you because of that. I need you, Francine.

FRANCINE. And you need Lizzie apparently.

MICHAEL. No. That's some stupid...I don't know what that is. That's a candy shop, that's a fudge factory, that's a diabetic seizure waiting to happen.

FRANCINE. *(laughs)* So, I'm, what, a meat and potatoes factory?

MICHAEL. You're the solid part. You're the banks of our river –

FRANCINE. Oh god.

MICHAEL. I'm sorry, I don't mean banks –

FRANCINE. I don't want to be the banks! I'm the banks for my sister's river, my father's river, everybody I know's damn river! I want to be the river once, Michael! I'm tired of being the sand and the rocks!

(beat)

MICHAEL. Okay. So. Stop.

FRANCINE. What?

MICHAEL. Stop being the rocks. You can be the water and I'll be the rock for a while.

FRANCINE. And how are you going to do that?

MICHAEL. I have no idea. I've never been a rock in my life. You can ask anyone.

FRANCINE. Yeah, well, I'm not used to...flowing. Or whatever it is water does.

(beat)

MICHAEL. You're already kind of doing it.

(*She looks at him.*)

You're not stopping Karen's river anymore.

(*She watches him…*)

FRANCINE. Can I have another bite of cookie?

(**MICHAEL** *grins. He starts to feed her…and a cell phone rings.* **MICHAEL** *and* **FRANCINE** *hesitate…it rings again…*)

MICHAEL & FRANCINE. Is that yours?

FRANCINE & MICHAEL. No.

(**LIZZIE** *runs in, followed by* **STUART** *[with a drink] and* **WALLY**.)

LIZZIE. Not my ringtone.

MICHAEL. (*overlapping*) Not mine.

FRANCINE. (*overlapping*) Not mine.

STUART. (*overlapping*) Not mine.

(*It rings again. They look to* **WALLY**.)

WALLY. I ain't even got a ringtone, so don't look at me.

(**FRANCINE** *looks around, finds a phone behind the flowers. It rings.*)

FRANCINE. Is this Karen's?

STUART. Must be.

FRANCINE. (*hands it to* **WALLY**) You answer it, Dad.

WALLY. Why me?

(*Ring*)

FRANCINE. It's your house.

WALLY. It's not my phone.

FRANCINE. It could be important!

WALLY. (*fumbling with the phone*) I don't, ah –

STUART. Press "Talk"

(**WALLY** *does.*)

WALLY. *(into phone)* Hello?

> *(They all wait.* **FRANCINE** *turns the phone over so* **WAL-LY**'s *speaking into the right end.)*

WALLY *(cont.) (into phone)* Hello?...No, this is her father. Who? Sure.

> *(hangs up)*

Crank call.

FRANCINE. Who was it?

WALLY. Said he was Max Aphelion, needed to talk to Karen.

FRANCINE. Dad!

MICHAEL. That's her fiancé!

WALLY. Her fiancé is already here!

LIZZIE & MICHAEL. What?

WALLY. I thought you all knew him.

> *(gestures to* **STUART***)*

This is the man Karen's going to marry.

> *(Beat...and* **STUART** *collapses to the couch.)*

FRANCINE. Oh my word!

LIZZIE. Ohmygod ohmygod ohmygod –

MICHAEL. Dude! Why didn't you tell us, buddy?

STUART. I...I didn't know...Mr. Baedeker, did Karen tell you this?

WALLY. Only about 16 dozen times.

STUART. Oh my god.

FRANCINE. Unbelievable.

MICHAEL. Congratulations, man!

LIZZIE. Super super super super –

WALLY. It's been Max this, Max that, I love Max, Max is the perfect man, Max Max Max.

> *(They all stare at him.)*

FRANCINE. This isn't Max, Dad.

MICHAEL. This is Stuart. Stuart Tramontane.

WALLY. Oh. *(beat)* Well. Better luck next time, son.

(**STUART** *slumps back on the couch.*)

LIZZIE. Bad bad bad bad bad –

MICHAEL. It's okay, man –

FRANCINE. You're better off, Stuart, you really are –

WALLY. *(calling off)* Karen, honey, I just hung up on your fiancé! I hope it wasn't important!

KAREN. *(offstage)* You WHAT??

(**FRANCINE** *takes the phone, punches in the call-back.*)

WALLY. You want me to e-mail him? I can e-mail him back –

LIZZIE. Karen's phone knows his number, it's okay.

FRANCINE. *(into phone)* Max? Hi, it's Francine, Karen's sister. Sorry about my dad. He gets confused.

WALLY. *(yelling to the phone)* He's a moron!

FRANCINE. *(into phone)* Where are you?

(pause, then calling out)

Karen!

MICHAEL. *(quietly)* What's going on?

FRANCINE. He wants to tell Karen.

LIZZIE. He can't, it's bad luck for the groom to talk to the bride before the wedding –

KAREN. *(offstage)* What, Francine?

WALLY. Max is on the phone for you!

MICHAEL. It's bad luck to *see* the bride, not talk to her on her cell.

STUART. *(to **FRANCINE**)* How's the reception?

*(And **KAREN** comes out. Nervous, in a simple white bridal gown. She looks…truly astonishing. Pause.)*

MICHAEL. Whoa.

WALLY. Oh, Karie.

STUART. Um.

LIZZIE. Oh. My. God.

FRANCINE. *(holds up the phone)* It's Max.

KAREN. *(fearfully steps up and takes the phone)* Hi, sweetheart. What's up? …okay. Um. I guess the good news? …Oh thank god. No, no, I wasn't doubting, I was just, of course you're coming! What's, what's the bad news? …You're still laid over in O'Hare?

FRANCINE. Oh god. O'Hare.

STUART. O'Hare.

MICHAEL. Never do O'Hare after 11 A.M.

STUART. He'll never get out of there.

FRANCINE. Did he knowingly schedule a plane change at O'Hare?

KAREN. He and his best man were delayed getting in, they missed their connection, the next flight is in…

(listening)

…another three hours?

FRANCINE. Oh lord.

MICHAEL. Then there's the fly time –

FRANCINE. And there's the drive time from the airport –

KAREN. He won't get here until 9 o'clock at the earliest.

(Beat. They all look at each other.)

FRANCINE. Our plane leaves for home at 8:30.

MICHAEL. I have to get back for a 6 A.M. flight to Memphis.

STUART. And I have to head out tonight at 9:15.

KAREN. Well then…

(They all watch her…)

Let's do it now.

STUART. What?

KAREN. If we get married now, I can drive down and meet him at the airport and we can have our honeymoon night at the Airport Ramada Inn.

STUART. Karen –

KAREN. I have to be back to work tomorrow anyway, we'll take a real honeymoon when our schedules line up

– listen, you all came here for a wedding, *I* came here for a wedding, Max is standing in O'Hare in a tuxedo for God's sake, and we are going to have a wedding –

STUART. Karen!

(He grabs the phone. They all look at him… KAREN realizes he's in the room for the first time.)

KAREN. Oh. Stuart.

STUART. Karen, I had to come. I just…are you totally, absolutely sure you want to do this?

(Beat. She watches him.)

KAREN. As sure as I've ever been of anything in my life.

FRANCINE. You had your "huh" moment.

KAREN. I did.

(Beat. To STUART)

I didn't choose it. But I've got to follow it.

(They look at each other…a moment more passes.)

STUART. You see, it's just… My whole life, my life after I met you, it was like I couldn't even get a signal from any other women because my channel is permanently tuned to "Karen": "Would Karen say that?" "I wonder if Karen feels that way too?" Which was stupid, because I clearly…I need to reposition my satellites. But I need to make absolutely in my gut sure you're not going to suddenly start sending out signals I'm going to miss the minute I reposition.

(Beat. She takes his hand.)

KAREN. I promise. It's okay for you to reposition your satellites.

*(Beat. They look at each other….**STUART** nods and hands her the phone.)*

STUART. Then you better get on with this. His roaming charges must be eating him alive.

*(He lets go of her hand as **LIZZIE** takes his other hand to gently help him step away.)*

KAREN. *(into phone)* Max, we're doing this over the phone. Can you hear me okay?

FRANCINE. And we're off!

LIZZIE. It's like delivering a baby in the back of a taxi cab –

STUART. Have you done that?

LIZZIE. Only twice. I'm a certified midwife.

MICHAEL. *(holding up his cell phone)* I'll be the photographer!

KAREN. Stuart, will you hold the phone?

STUART. *(taking the cell)* Story of my life –

(**MICHAEL** *now is circling around recording everything on his phone.*)

KAREN. Francine? Dad?

(She gestures for them to join her to one side.)

WALLY. Don't this beat the nuts off a monkey.

(They all get in position, **LIZZIE** *pulls out cards with notes on them to read. It's a perfectly traditional wedding tableau, but with a cell phone being held up where the groom would stand.)*

LIZZIE. Um. Okay. Wow. Okay. Um –

(reading)

"Dearly Beloved, we are gathered here today to join this woman and this... man – in holy matrimony."

(into phone)

Can you hear me okay, Max?

(They all listen... she nods and carries on.)

"If any person can show just cause why they may not be joined together..."

(She looks at **FRANCINE** *and* **STUART**... *who pause... contain themselves.)*

"Then that person should just keep their causes to themselves. Marriage is a union of husband and wife, in heart, body, and mind...once they are in the same county."

KAREN. *(quietly)* Lizzie…

LIZZIE. I'm sorry. "Who gives this woman in marriage to this man?"

WALLY. Me. I do. And her mother does. With the greatest joy in the world.

(KAREN beams at WALLY. FRANCINE grins and squeezes her father's hand.)

LIZZIE. "Do you, Max Aphelion, take Karen Baedeker to be your wife, to love, comfort, and honor her in sickness and in health, for richer, for poorer, for better, for worse, as long as you both shall live?"

(They listen to the phone. Apparently he does.)

"And do you, Karen Baedeker, take Max Aphelion to be your husband, to love, comfort, and honor him in sickness and in health, for richer, for poorer, for better, for worse, as long as you both shall live?"

KAREN. I do.

LIZZIE. What token of love do you offer?

(Beat. They look around…)

KAREN. Oh no. He's got the rings. He's very traditional, he's got the rings –

LIZZIE. *(into phone)* Do you have the rings with you in O'Hare, Max?

WALLY. Here!

(Pulls a ring off his own finger.)

Use this.

(KAREN hesitates.)

It brought me a better life than I had any right to expect. Use it to start yours. You can give it back after later.

KAREN. Thank you.

(She takes the ring.)

LIZZIE. We're good. "In placing this ring, this symbol of unity, on this finger, you are pledging your love from this day forward." Are you putting on a ring there, Max?

*(Beat. **LIZZIE** nods.)*

"Then what God and Verizon have joined together let no man put asunder. And so by the power invested in me, I now pronounce you husband and wife. You may kiss the phone.

*(Another cell phone rings. **FRANCINE, MICHAEL,** and **STUART** instinctively about to check…hesitate. **STUART** glances at his, embarrassed.)*

STUART. Shoot, it's my boss.

*(Another phone rings – **MICHAEL** looks at his –)*

MICHAEL. It's work. Dang it –

*(Another ring – **FRANCINE** looks at her phone.)*

FRANCINE. I do not believe this. It's a client…

(The phones ring again…)

WALLY. Of for God's sake, people, don't any of you have, whatdoyoucallit – voice mail??

(They pause…nod and click their phones off.)

*(**KAREN** grins at them all…and takes the phone from **STUART,** tossing him the bouquet. He catches it. Blinks. **LIZZIE** grins and kisses him. He looks at her.)*

STUART. Huh.

*(**KAREN** smiles and kisses her cell phone lovingly. They all clap, **FRANCINE** throws rose petals, the three couples beaming, it's a perfect traditional tableau…except for the cell-phone-groom part. The happiest techno version of the Wedding March plays.)*

(And we…blackout.)

End of Play

OTHER TITLES AVAILABLE FROM SAMUEL FRENCH

MAURITIUS
Theresa Rebeck

Comedy / 3m, 2f / Interior

Stamp collecting is far more risky than you think. After their mother's death, two estranged half-sisters discover a book of rare stamps that may include the crown jewel for collectors. One sister tries to collect on the windfall, while the other resists for sentimental reasons. In this gripping tale, a seemingly simple sale becomes dangerous when three seedy, high-stakes collectors enter the sisters' world, willing to do anything to claim the rare find as their own.

"(Theresa Rebeck's) belated Broadway bow, the only original
play by a woman to have its debut on Broadway this fall."
- Robert Simonson, *New York Times*

"*Mauritius* caters efficiently to a hunger that Broadway hasn't
been gratifying in recent years. That's the corkscrew-twist drama
of suspense… she has strewn her script with a multitude of
mysteries."
- Ben Brantley, *New York Times*

"Theresa Rebeck is a slick playwright… Her scenes have a crisp
shape, her dialogue pops, her characters swagger through an
array of showy emotion, and she knows how to give a plot
a cunning twist."
- John Lahr, *The New Yorker*

For me to do:
- ring door bell p.42
                    P.62 twice
                    P.63
                    P.65

- Music at the end

- Tell about hall right
- change in lines and
  when read

CPSIA information can be obtained at www.ICGtesting.com
Printed in the USA
LVOW071113121212

311296LV00003B/185/P

9 780573 663987